THE BRITISH DESTROYER

By the same author

BRITISH WARSHIP NAMES

(with Cdr. C. F. Walker)

HORNET ON HER TRIALS

DIAMOND ON HER TRIALS, 1952

THE
BRITISH
DESTROYER

CAPTAIN T. D. MANNING
C.B.E., V.R.D., R.N.V.R. (*Ret'd*)

GODFREY CAVE ASSOCIATES

© *Captain T. D. Manning* 1961

First published in Great Britain in 1961
by Putnam & Co Ltd
42 *Great Russell Street, London*
and printed for the publishers by
Ebenezer Baylis and Son, Limited
The Trinity Press, Worcester, and London

This facsimile edition
first published 1979 *by*
Godfrey Cave Associates Ltd
42 *Bloomsbury Street,*
London WC1B 3QJ
and also printed by
Ebenezer Baylis and Son, Limited

ISBN 0 906223 13 X

CONTENTS

LIST OF ILLUSTRATIONS

FOREWORD

THE original title of the destroyer was "torpedo-boat destroyer" but the function of the type has long since been merged into that of the torpedo-boat. The title "destroyer", however, has stuck and has always appealed to the imagination. The low profile and black paint of the boats of the early part of the century gave way to something bigger until finality was reached with the monstrous "D" class of the late 1940s. These vessels are miniature cruisers and have been named, officially, "*Daring* class ships", though now they are again known as destroyers.

The torpedo-boat destroyer shed the first part of her title in the Navy Lists of 1925 and became a destroyer. The style T.B.D. of earlier days lingered for some time and may even now be used by the elderly, but its significance lapsed many years ago.

It was in the First World War that the destroyer became a "maid of all work" and her value as a convoy escort and anti-submarine vessel was realized. Her function as a fleet destroyer remained, but with the disappearance of the battle fleet many destroyers have changed their rating to frigate and now that misused title signifies not only anti-submarine vessels but also anti-aircraft and aircraft-direction ships as well. As the cruiser—the true frigate—seems to be on the way out, perhaps the modern frigate does now fulfil the functions of the type in this modern age.

One of the most absurd misnomers of our day is that of "Guided missile destroyer" which obviously signifies a vessel which destroys guided missiles. These are to be large vessels of about 5,000 tons and must come within the cruiser range.

Being now the "poor relation" of the U.S. Navy, we have had to alter our historic term "flotilla" as a collective noun for small craft and we now refer to destroyer squadrons. It seems a pity. But in an age when the ancient word "heads" has been replaced by "toilets", anything can happen.

After the naval manœuvres of 1890, it was pointed out that the value of torpedo-boat operations for training purposes was very great. Some doubts were expressed whether such experience could replace early training in the manipulation of masts and sails which, it was generally acknowledged, gave our sailors the necessary skill, nerve and resource needed to produce true seamen, but it was said that a certain period in torpedo-boats was an essential part of a naval education. It is interesting to find that one objection was raised because service in these craft tended to absolve the crew from strictly observing naval regulations!

Large numbers of officers served in destroyers during the years before 1914 and, during the First World War, these officers were needed to command the many boats built in the war years. In the years between the wars, destroyers became larger and more complicated; promotion was hard to come by and the old type of care-free destroyer officer disappeared, yet a new type was created who did magnificently between 1939 and 1946. But the old destroyer "character" has gone.

Gone are the times when the destroyers of the early days crowded to-gether in the Pens at Portland and Port Edgar, in the Pockets at Gibraltar and in Sliema Creek at Malta, when each boat had three or four officers and flotillas were twenty strong. To appreciate the spirit of the old destroyer service the reader should turn to "Flotillas" by Lionel Dawson and "Endless Story" by Taffrail. The daring and self-reliance derived from massed attacks and night attacks produced a type of officer of the highest quality. In those days, unhappily gone for ever it seems, the endless paper work of a later age was virtually non-existent.

If a 1911 Navy List is consulted it will be found that the torpedo-boats were commanded by lieutenants of two years' seniority and upwards. There were 44 boats commanded by lieutenants of five years' seniority and another 25 by those with five or six years in. For the most part, the more junior officers commanded the older boats, the more modern "oily-wads" were given to the more senior.

Of the destroyers, apart from those commanded by commanders, we find the number of boats commanded by lieutenants works out as follows:

9–13 years' seniority	.. ..	32
8 years' seniority	.. ..	28
7 years' seniority	.. ..	28
6 years' seniority	.. ..	25
Less than 6 years' seniority	..	14

Here again, the destroyers serving in full commission in the Home Fleet were given to the more senior officers; those in commission with reduced crews were the training ground for a large number of more junior lieutenants. It must be remembered that the rank of Lieut.-Commander had not been introduced and that promotion to Commander was earlier than it was between the wars.

While many officers who served in destroyers continued to do so, almost uninterruptedly, there were also large numbers who served in them during the annual manœuvres so that experience in small craft was widely spread among the non-specialist officers (known as "Salt horse") in the Navy.

In this book I have tried to give a description of destroyers from the *Havock* to the *Daring* class. I have not attempted to go into great detail nor will the full war services and battle honours of the later destroyers be found. In "British Warship Names", written by Commander C. F. Walker and myself, all battle honours will be found, but I have referred shortly to U-boat "kills".

In order to make the book what might be called "a textbook on destroyers" I have illustrated it as fully as possible and if I have seemed to devote a good deal of space to the first twenty or thirty years of the type, I have done so because I feel that the earlier destroyers were of such great interest and variety. I am indebted to my old friend Mr. Richard Perkins whose photographs I have used extensively. He and I wrote a book about destroyers in 1938; it never saw the light of day but I have been able to use much of the material we collected over twenty years ago.

ACKNOWLEDGEMENTS

I AM grateful to the following for the help they have given me with this book.

Lieut.-Commander P. K. Kemp, F.S.A., R.N. (Ret.), the Admiralty Archivist, and the staff of the Historical Section.

The Director of Ships and the Material Branch of the Admiralty.

Lieut.-Commander Arthur Waite, R.N.R., Mr. Michael Robinson and the staff of the National Maritime Museum.

The Keeper of Photographs at the Imperial War Museum.

My old friends Mr. Derisley Trimingham and Mr. W. P. Trotter, M.C.

Messrs. John I. Thornycroft & Co. Ltd.

Messrs. Yarrow & Co. Ltd.

The General Manager of Palmer's Hebburn Works.

Messrs. Vickers-Armstrong Limited.

Messrs. J. Samuel White & Co. Ltd.

Messrs. John Brown & Co. (Clydebank) Ltd.

Lastly, a number of Naval Officers, serving and retired, who would, I know, prefer to remain anonymous.

THE BRITISH DESTROYER

DESTROYER NAMES

WHO chose the names of the early destroyers cannot now be ascertained but a study of the names shows that almost all were old small-ship names which had tradition behind them. In fact, up to the time of the "Rivers", only ten names were new to the Service, mostly fish names. It is true that they were a pretty varied lot and some might seem a trifle inappropriate; *Dove*, for example, sounds ridiculous for a destroyer but the name referred to the river, not to the gentle bird! I think it unlikely that it was pronounced as it should be however.

The majority of the "River" names were used for the first time, only six being traditional. There were several in use already, *Leven*, *Dove*, *Avon* and *Lee* for example, but when a new type is introduced, it is perfectly reasonable to bring in new names. Since then, many of the names have been revived, first for trawlers after the First World War and then for frigates in the Second. They have thus established themselves in our naval traditions.

The first "Tribals" were a mixed bag; some of them, such as *Crusader* and *Viking*, can hardly be called tribal names for it cannot be thought that the Crusaders of the Middle Ages would be flattered if they had been described as a tribe! In the *Beagle* class there were no new names at all and most of them had been borne six or eight times before. The same applies to the *Acorn* and *Acheron* classes; all these names were well chosen. With the "K" class (*Acasta*, etc.) we find some old destroyer names such as *Ardent*, *Shark*, *Contest*, *Sparrowhawk* and *Spitfire* being revived. Four destroyers have been named *Shark*.

In 1913, Mr. Churchill, who was the First Lord, appointed a committee to investigate destroyer names and their classification. This committee was under the chairmanship of Captain H. Lynes, R.N., and performed the task with great thoroughness. The principal recommendation was that all destroyers should be classified by letters, the "A" class being the 27-knotters, the "B", "C" and "D" classes were the four-, three- and two-funnelled 30-knotters, the "Rivers" were the "E" class, the "Tribals" were "F", the *Acorns* "H", the *Acherons* "I" and the *Acastas* "K". Why J was omitted is not known though it is possible that the committee's final suggestion may have made them shy of finding enough names.

The recommendation was that all existing destroyers should be renamed with their class letters and lists were prepared of suitable names which, the committee said, were "historic, appropriate, harmonious and not absurd". What fun they must have had!

Their lordships, quite rightly, refused to accept this suggestion for it involved renaming destroyers, some of which had been in commission for many years. The confusion would have been frightful and the signal books would have been a mass of corrections.

But the Admiralty accepted the proposals, apart from this, and the new lettering system was introduced with the "L" class, none of which had been launched, and it has lasted ever since with the exception of special classes such as the "Tribals" and "Battles". On the whole, the new "L" names were better than those originally selected though a few old destroyer names were lost when the *Daring*, *Haughty*, *Havock*, *Dragon* and *Rocket* were renamed. Only nine of the "L" names had been borne before, but this is only to be expected when a large class is named with the same initial letter.

The same thing happened all through the war, though when the post-war destroyers came along, there being only eight in each class, there was no excuse for introducing new names. In fact, until the *Escapade* of the "E" class of 1934, all names had been traditional. So it went on; *Hereward*, though new to the Service, was an appropriate name and three of the "I" class names were new, but this is a difficult letter. When the "J" class names were announced, all those interested in ship names were horrified to see *Jubilant* in the list! Mercifully, this boat was never built as it was decided to have the leader as one of the eight.

Seven of the eight "K" names were new but they were all quite appropriate, though some people thought that the leader, *Kelly*, was named in honour of a too recent admiral. In modern times it has been the custom to allow a decent interval to elapse between the death of a naval worthy and the naming of a ship after him. This was seen in the cases of the *Jellicoe* and *Beatty*.

The new "Tribals" revived some of the original names but many of them were new. Two tribal names were given to destroyers of the "L" and "M" classes. When the *Gurkha* of 1937 was lost in 1940, the Gurkha regiments subscribed a day's pay per man to pay for a new ship and the *Larne* was renamed. Similarly, the *Marksman* of 1941 was renamed *Mahratta* as a gesture to the warlike Indian regiments.

The wartime destroyers built under the supplementary war programmes continued the lettered system though at one time it seemed likely that the flotillas would catch up with their own tail, so to speak. When the Ships' Names Committee took over in 1940, they found that the "O" to "R" classes had already been named, but one name they could not stomach and this was *Persistent* so one of their first acts was to rename her the *Petard*, a Jutland name.

The committee had difficulty in approving the eight "Q" names already chosen, six being new to the Service including, curiously enough, *Quiberon*. But as no better alternatives suggested themselves, these names were allowed to stand and attention was turned to finding good names for the "S" class. There was no difficulty in selecting old names for all new destroyers down to the "W" class though the system of giving the leader a distinguished naval officer's name of the same initial broke down when the "U" class was reached. The committee rather prided themselves on finding traditional "Z" names for all but one of that flotilla.

There seemed no end in sight to the building of new destroyers, all of which were of the "O" to "Z" or intermediate type, so it was decided to abandon the batches of eight and simply give names in the "O" to "Z" range, but it was then found that the next lot of four flotillas were to be different and so the committee named them the Co-, Cr-, Ch- and Ca-classes, there being no "C" class in the Royal Navy. The four boats which had been in the "C" half-flotilla had all been transferred to Canada in 1937–38.

The next destroyers were to be larger and, in relation to the four "C" flotillas, they compared as did the second "Tribals" to the "A" to "I" classes. So it was decided to break the alphabetical system and name these new vessels after battles. There followed the "Weapon" class of which only four were built. Thereafter it was decided to revert to letters once more and two classes of "D" destroyers and one of "G" were named. The end of the war caused the cancellation of half the "D's" and all the "G's". The letters "A" and "B" had been appropriated for submarines, though the latter boats were never built.

Flotilla leaders at first were built in classes and during the First World War a number of them were named after admirals. One class was named after

Scottish clans. After the war, when the new flotillas of eight were built, a leader was provided for each flotilla, those for the "A", "B" and "C" flotillas being the *Codrington*, *Keith* and *Kempenfelt*. With the "D" class, however, the leader was named after a naval worthy whose name began with the class letter.

The "Hunt" class which became known as destroyers until re-classified as frigates, caused some difficulties as a good many of the names of Hunts were unknown to the simple sailor. However, they were not too bad though it is as well the type was not continued indefinitely.

In 1940, when the fifty American "four-stackers" were transferred to the Royal Navy, Captain Tapprell Dorling, D.S.O., R.N. (Taffrail) hit upon the idea of renaming them with town names common to both Great Britain (and the Commonwealth) and the U.S.A. Some of the names were traditional, four of them having been borne five times before (*Lancaster*, *Richmond*, *St. Albans* and *Salisbury*).

It is a point of interest that fifty of the names chosen by the Ships' Names Committee had been previously borne by destroyers.

DESTROYER BUILDERS

THE original builders, as has been said in the remarks about the early destroyers, were Yarrow and Thornycroft, or to be more precise, Yarrow & Co. Ltd., Scotstoun, Glasgow, and John I. Thornycroft & Co. Ltd., originally at Chiswick and later at Woolston, Southampton. The early Yarrow boats were built at Poplar, but in 1906 the yard moved to Scotstoun.

Another firm early in the field with destroyers was Cammell Laird & Co. Ltd., Birkenhead, whose early boats were distinguished by their funnels extending farther aft because the engine room was between the two boiler rooms. William Doxford and Sons Limited of Sunderland built a number of destroyers, starting in 1895. The Fairfield Shipbuilding and Engineering Co. Ltd. of Glasgow were also among the early builders and continued to build destroyers for many years. Palmer's Shipbuilding and Engineering Co. Ltd. of Hebburn-on-Tyne launched their first boat in 1895. Many of the early boats built by this firm had funnel capes for which a reason is put forward on page 45, but it is not certain that this is the correct explanation, for the builders say that the reason may have been to prevent rain and sea water washing the soot from the funnels down the casing.

The Clydebank Engineering Co. Ltd. launched their first destroyer in 1894. This firm became John Brown & Co. Ltd. in 1899. Destroyers built by them are always known as Clydebank boats.

J. Samuel White & Co. Ltd. of Cowes, Isle of Wight, were one of the earliest firms to build torpedo craft and have built many destroyers for the Royal Navy. About 1917-19 a number of their destroyers had distinctive ribbed funnels the purpose of which was to strengthen the thin steel which was used to save weight.

A few destroyers were built by Earle's Shipbuilding and Engineering Co. of Hull and a few others by Hanna Donald and Wilson of Paisley. R. & W. Hawthorn, Leslie & Co. Ltd. of Hebburn-on-Tyne have built many destroyers and have a good reputation in the Service. Their boats have had most distinctive funnel tops, parallel to the deck and with prominent cages. Vickers Limited of Barrow-in-Furness have built destroyers from the early days both before and after amalgamation with Armstrong Whitworth. Boats noted as being "Elswick" were built by Sir W. G. Armstrong, Whitworth & Co. Ltd. at their yard at Elswick on the Tyne. This firm became known as Vickers-Armstrong in 1908.

Denny & Co., Dumbarton, built their first destroyer in 1908–09 but since then they have built many more. The London and Glasgow Engineering and Iron Shipbuilding Co. Ltd. of Govan launched their first in 1910 and built a few more. Another firm which built a few destroyers was A. & J. Inglis Limited of Glasgow while Swan, Hunter and Wigham Richardson, of Wallsend-on-Tyne, have built many boats in the last forty years.

During the First World War, and shortly before then, a number of destroyers was built by William Beardmore & Co. Ltd. at Dalmuir, on the Clyde; another new-comer to this type of work was Alex. Stephen & Co. Ltd. of Govan, who has built a good many boats since the First War.

Another firm to take on destroyer building during the First World War was Harland and Wolff Limited who have built this type of craft at their Govan Yard. During the war, too, Scott's Shipbuilding and Engineering Co. Ltd. began the building of destroyers at their yard at Greenock.

In the pages which follow, the names of the firms which built the destroyers are shortened to the form by which they have always been familiarly known. This chapter has been included to give some idea of these firms and also their full titles.

ANTI-SUBMARINE WEAPONS

THE standard weapon against a submerged submarine ever since the First World War until comparatively recently was the depth-charge. The difficulty, however, was to locate the enemy and the best device used up to 1918 was the Hydrophone which was not accurately directional, and therefore it was essential to sight the submarine in order to attack it, or else follow up a torpedo track.

At the end of the war the Asdic was being developed, so called after the Allied Submarine Detection Investigation Committee. During the years following the war, the Royal Navy continued to carry out research though only the Americans pursued the investigations on their own lines.

About 1923–24, the first four running destroyers, of the 6th Flotilla, were fitted with Asdics and after extensive trials the equipment was fitted into all new construction as well as the running flotillas. The offensive weapon was still the depth-charge discharged from chutes in the stern and throwers which fired over the side. But the attack was not really precise as there was time for a submarine to take violent evading action in the interval between an unavoidable loss of Asdic contact at close range and the time of explosion of the charges. Nevertheless, this method of attack proved very successful in the early days of the war.

The next stage was to cut out the time gap referred to above and in order to do this it was seen that the chances of success would be enhanced if the charges could be thrown ahead of the attacking ship before contact was lost. The first weapon designed for the purpose was known as the Hedgehog which was a spigot mortar firing ahead from a position on the forecastle; twenty-four bombs were discharged which exploded on contact with the target.

Before long, the Hedgehog was improved on and a new ahead-throwing weapon, the Squid, was produced. This fired heavy charges in salvoes of three and could be fired from a position in the stern if necessary as the missiles went sufficiently high in the air to clear masts and bridge. The Squid, in its turn, has been improved on by Limbo which hardly enters into our orbit as it is not fitted in destroyers but only in frigates. Both these weapons are synchronized with the Asdic set and their operation is fully automatic.

DESTROYER FLOTILLAS

UP to 1905, all destroyers were based on the Home Ports with the exception of those on foreign service. The Channel Flotilla came into being in 1905 and there was also, for a short time, an Atlantic Fleet Flotilla. The Home Fleet Flotillas at the Home Ports were in commission with nucleus crews and supplied boats as tenders to establishments, and other miscellaneous services. There was also a Home Fleet Flotilla in commission with full crews.

In 1909, the Channel Fleet was abolished and the Home Fleet Flotilla was divided into the 1st and 2nd Flotillas which also included some boats from the old Channel Fleet. The 3rd Division of the Home Fleet embraced all other destroyers at Home and were in commission with nucleus crews. The 1st Flotilla consisted of the "Tribals" and "River" classes, while the 2nd Flotilla consisted mainly of "Rivers". As they were completed, the "G" class destroyers passed into the 1st Flotilla (except four which went to the 2nd) and from 1910 the "Rivers" of the 2nd Flotilla were replaced by the "H" class. At this time the 1st and 2nd Flotillas consisted of about 24 boats each. Meanwhile, the 3rd Fleet Flotilla had been numbered; the 3rd at the Nore, 4th at Portsmouth and the 5th at Devonport. In 1911 a new flotilla, the 7th, was formed from the "I" class as they passed into service.

There was a further reorganization in 1912 when the 1st Flotilla consisted of the "I" class, the 2nd of the "H" class, the 3rd of the "G" class and the 4th of the "K" class as they were completed. In 1913, the "G" class boats were transferred to the Mediterranean as the 5th Flotilla and their place was taken by the "Tribals" and, later, by the "L" class. In 1912 older destroyers were formed into the Patrol Flotillas under the Admiral of Patrols and were numbered 6th (Portsmouth), 7th (Devonport), 8th and 9th (The Nore).

In 1914, when war broke out, the 1st, 2nd, and 4th Flotillas were part of the Grand Fleet, the 3rd Flotilla became the Harwich Force, the 6th Flotilla went to Dover, the 7th to the East Coast; the 8th and 9th were attached to the Grand Fleet for patrol duties.

The 1st Flotilla remained with the Grand Fleet until late in 1916 when they became attached to the 3rd Battle Squadron. In the spring of 1917 the flotilla was transferred to Portsmouth but later in the year the "I" class boats went to the Mediterranean and were replaced by some "L" class and, later, "River" class boats.

The 2nd Flotilla remained with the Grand Fleet until the spring of 1916 when it was transferred to Devonport until the autumn of 1917. There was then a reorganization whereby the 2nd and 4th Flotillas were merged into the 2nd, stationed at Buncrana in Northern Ireland. The majority of the "H" class boats went to the Mediterranean. The 2nd Flotilla remained at Buncrana until the end of the war and eventually consisted of a variety of boats, largely "G" class.

The 3rd Flotilla remained at Harwich until the summer of 1915 when it was renumbered the 9th. A new 3rd Flotilla was formed in the spring of 1918 and was attached to the Grand Fleet. It was made up of "M" class boats.

The 4th Flotilla remained with the Grand Fleet until the late summer of 1916 when it moved to the Humber. It then, at the end of the year, moved to Portsmouth and, in the spring of 1917, to Devonport. Later in 1917, the 2nd Flotilla joined the 4th, the latter remaining at Devonport.

The 6th Flotilla was at Dover throughout the war and consisted mainly of "Tribals" and 30-knotters, though other types joined from time to time.

The 7th Flotilla was on the East Coast all the war, the 9th being merged into it in the autumn of 1915. In the summer of 1917 it became known as the East Coast Convoys, 7th Flotilla.

The 8th Flotilla was stationed in the Firth of Forth until the spring of 1918 when it was abolished.

The 9th Flotilla was on the East Coast until the autumn of 1915 when it joined with the 7th. It was then reconstituted as part of the Harwich Force with boats of the 3rd Flotilla. In the spring of 1917 it was merged into the 10th Flotilla and all "L" boats were withdrawn.

The 10th Flotilla was formed in the spring of 1915 at Harwich with boats of the early "M" class which were later relieved by "R" class and combined with the 9th Flotilla in the spring of 1917.

The 11th Flotilla was constituted with "M" class boats as a Grand Fleet Flotilla in the autumn of 1915. "R" class boats joined later but by the end of the war it consisted almost entirely of "V" and "W" boats.

The 12th Flotilla was constituted with "M" class boats as a part of the Grand Fleet late in 1915. In 1918, the older boats were replaced by "S" and a few "W" class.

The 13th Flotilla was formed as a Grand Fleet Flotilla in the spring of 1916 with "M" class boats which were replaced from the summer of 1917 onwards by modified "R", "V" and "W" boats.

The 14th Flotilla was formed in the summer of 1916 and was attached to the Grand Fleet. It consisted of "M" class boats but at the end of the war units of the "S", "V" and "W" classes began to join.

The 15th, and last of the Grand Fleet Flotillas, was formed with "R" class boats in the autumn of 1916.

In addition to the various local defence flotillas round the ports of the United Kingdom, there were 29 destroyers attached to the Grand Fleet in 1914 for local defence and patrol duties. During the war the flotilla was gradually reduced until the last three boats were removed in April 1918.

Destroyers were sent to the Mediterranean in 1895, and ever since then there have been from one to four flotillas on the station. Various boats of the 27- and 30-knotter types served there but in 1911 the older boats were withdrawn and relieved by "River" class. In 1913, the "G" class of 16 boats went to the Mediterranean and remained there until 1917 when most of them returned home. By this time a number of the "H" and "I" classes had arrived on the station. A few of the "River" class had been in the 5th Flotilla (as it was known from 1913) since early in 1915. This flotilla is very difficult to follow as destroyers were attached to the Adriatic Squadron from time to time and, in the autumn of 1917, a Malta Flotilla was formed which, a few months later, was merged into the 5th until July 1918 when the main flotilla was moved to Brindisi.

The first destroyers went to China in 1898. A division of "Rivers" went out for a time in 1905 and in 1911 more of the class went out to relieve the older boats. These were followed by four more in 1913 but after the fall of Tsing-tao, all the "Rivers" joined the Mediterranean Fleet.

1919-39

AFTER the war, the Grand Fleet was abolished and the Atlantic Fleet came into being. Four destroyer flotillas (1st to 4th) were formed, each of 16

"V" and "W" boats with two divisions of "S" class in the 4th. Twenty "S" class boats were stationed in the Mediterranean and formed the 6th Flotilla, one division being in reserve. The majority of the "M" destroyers and all pre-war boats were laid up and prepared for sale to the shipbreakers. The "R" class, and many of the "S" class, were in reserve.

In 1921 (or late 1920) the flotillas were reorganized, the Atlantic Fleet consisting of the 1st to 6th and 9th (reduced crews) each flotilla now being 8 destroyers and a leader. The "S" boats in the Mediterranean were numbered the 7th Flotilla. At this stage there were no destroyers on the China station, our arrangement with the U.S.A. being to maintain a submarine flotilla there while they provided destroyers.

During the next few years there were several changes in the numbering and composition of destroyer flotillas. In 1923 the "S" boats of the Mediterranean Fleet were replaced by modified "V" and "W" class and numbered 3rd and 4th, but the Atlantic Fleet destroyers were still composed of the original "V" and "W" class.

In 1925, the 1st and 2nd Flotillas went to the Mediterranean, making four flotillas on the station, while the Atlantic Fleet consisted of four flotillas, only two of which, the 5th and 6th, were in full commission. From 1926–28, the 3rd Flotilla was sent to China temporarily to help during the troubles there. It was this that proved the need for destroyers on the station and in 1927 the 8th Flotilla, consisting of the *Bruce* and eight "S" class boats, went to the Far East.

About this time, a centralized reserve of destroyers was established, known as the Maintenance Reserve, at Rosyth. It was designed to economize in manpower, the majority of the boats having no crews and others being in nominal commission only. Naturally, the state of efficiency was bound to drop and the boats, for the most part, were scrapped before their time.

In 1930, the new destroyers of the "A" class came into commission and became the 3rd Flotilla in the Mediterranean Fleet, followed a year later by the "B" class which formed the 4th Flotilla.

In 1932, the "S" class destroyers of the 8th (China) Flotilla were relieved by boats of the modified "W" class and the new "C" class, of which there were only four, joined the 2nd Flotilla of the Atlantic Fleet, with four "V" class. The Mediterranean Fleet was reduced by one flotilla, but the 1st Flotilla now (1933) consisted of the eight "D" class so that the fleet was made up of three flotillas of modern destroyers.

By 1935, the 5th Flotilla of the Home Fleet (late Atlantic) consisted of the

"E" class and the 6th Flotilla of the "F" class but the 8th Flotilla in China had changed places with the "D" boats in the Mediterranean and had become the 1st Flotilla. In 1935, two new flotillas were formed at Home, the 20th and 21st, both of "V" and "W" boats. The new destroyers of the "G" class at first formed the 20th Flotilla but in 1936 they became the 1st Flotilla of the Mediterranean Fleet. There was also a 19th Flotilla on that station, made up of a mixture of "V", "W" and "R" class boats. This was during the Italo-Abyssinian troubles but by the end of 1936 the flotillas were as follows: Home Fleet, 4th ("B" class); 5th ("E" class); 6th ("F" class): Mediterranean, 1st ("G" class); 2nd ("H" class); 3rd ("A" class): China, 8th ("D" class).

In 1937, the "A" class boats of the 3rd Flotilla were relieved by the new "I" class, the older boats going into reserve or employed on miscellaneous duties. At the end of 1938 and during 1939, the "Tribal" destroyers, as they completed, formed the 1st and 2nd Tribal Destroyer Flotillas, soon redesignated 6th (Home) and 4th (Mediterranean) destroyer flotillas. The new "J" class relieved the "E" boats in the 7th Flotilla (renumbered in 1939) and the "K" class formed the 5th Flotilla.

The war years are not recorded as the movements of destroyers were so varied and flotillas so seldom worked together as such. From the official history of the war at sea it is seen that the following was the distribution of destroyers at the outbreak of war.

Home Fleet	6th and 8th Flotillas. ("Tribals" and "F" class)
Channel Fleet	18th Flotilla. ("A" and "W" class)
Humber Force	7th Flotilla. ("J" class)
Plymouth	11th and 17th Flotillas. ("V" and "W" class)
Portland	12th Flotilla. ("E" class)
Rosyth and Milford Haven	15th Flotilla. ("W" class)
Portsmouth	16th Flotilla. ("S", "V" and "A" classes)
Dover	19th Flotilla. ("B" and "W" class)
Mediterranean	1st, 2nd, 3rd and 4th Flotillas. ("G", "H", "I" and "Tribal" classes)
North Atlantic	13th Flotilla. ("V" and "W" class)
China	21st Flotilla. (Ordered to the Mediterranean.) ("D" class)
South Atlantic	One division of the 2nd Flotilla. ("H" class)

The 5th Flotilla ("K" class) was in process of formation.

THE ILLUSTRATIONS

I HAVE done my best to vary the periods so that some of the more general alterations, which applied to many boats, can be seen. In the pre-1914 destroyers, some of the earlier styles of painting may be seen; other photographs show the 1908–12 appearance, while yet others show the 1914 or war-time changes.

In the later classes, I have included some pictures of boats as they appeared in the 1930s, several war-time photographs and a few, for the sake of completeness, after conversion to frigates or radar pickets. In this way I hope I have covered most periods, from trials to last days.

The wealth of material available made the selection very difficult and I am bound to confess that in some cases I have chosen photographs of which I am particularly fond. Most classes could be illustrated by quite a number of photographs showing the various changes made; however the size and cost of such a "picture book" of destroyers would, I fear, be prohibitive. But it would have been a delightful task.

There are several sources of supply. The collection of the Imperial War Museum is a very fine one and includes all the photographs taken by Symonds & Co. of Portsmouth, before the First World War, as well as the many official war photographs. The National Maritime Museum possesses a large collection but many of them are duplicates of pictures by other photographers.

Mr. Richard Perkins is not only an expert photographer but is also a collector and a real authority on identification. He has bought up the negatives of several photographers notably those of Ernest Hopkins of Southsea, who took a great many photographs in his day. Mr. Perkins's larger negatives are now in the possession of the Oscar Parkes Society which has also bought up the stock of Abrahams and Sons of Devonport.

Other photographers with good collections are Wright and Logan of Southsea, Skyfotos of Lympne Airport, A. and J. Pavia of Malta, P. A.

Vicary of Cromer and the Nautical Photograph Agency of Beccles. And there are, of course, others, but we seem to have lost access to one of the finest collections of negatives in existence, that of Richard Ellis of Malta. Material Branch of the Admiralty have a fine collection of official photographs which are available to the public.

One or two photographs in this book are unusual; the picture of the *Fervent* as completed with only one funnel is, to the best of my belief, unique for I have never seen another. Photographs of the *Ardent* and *Fortune* of 1913 are also very rare. For many years we searched for a photograph of the *Cobra* and two were at last discovered by Mr. W. P. Trotter, one of which he has kindly made available to me for this book.

All photographs are copyright.

THE DEVELOPMENT OF
DESTROYERS

THE building of large numbers of small torpedo-boats caused considerable alarm in naval circles. The historic idea of blockade still persisted and it was realized that a blockading fleet, close inshore, would be in grave danger from enemy torpedo-boats. Hence the creation of two types: 1st class torpedo-boats which were sea-going and were expected to act as a defence against the 2nd class boats which were purely for harbour defence. These 2nd class boats were also carried in most big ships in the eighties presumably for offensive operations on an enemy coast.

Our first torpedo-boat, the *Lightning* (later T.B.1) was launched in 1877. She was very small and carried one torpedo tube only. Many others followed. The 1st class T.B. laid down in 1885 were intended to act, not as torpedo-boats, but as "catchers" and the fleet was to be surrounded by a cordon of these boats as a protection against the coast defence T.B. of the enemy. However, once the war scare died down, these boats were armed with torpedoes instead of guns. Moreover, as the need for bigger and better torpedo-boat catchers was realized, it was decided to build vessels of a new type. The first of these was the *Rattlesnake*, launched by Laird in 1886, followed soon afterwards by three more. The *Rattlesnake* was designed for $18\frac{1}{2}$ knots, which speed she could always make, and the idea was to have vessels which could keep at sea in bad weather when the 1st class torpedo-boats were most uncomfortable, mount an armament which could sink enemy T.B. and have sufficient speed to overtake their quarry. These ships were known sometimes as "catchers" and sometimes as "torpedo gunboats" but before long, when it was found that the type was a failure, the latter term was adopted finally. A good many were built but, even after being re-boiled with water-tube boilers, few could make twenty knots. Most of the

IA. *KEMPENFELT, MOUNSEY* AND *ROB ROY* AT SEA

IB. *KEMPENFELT* AND DESTROYERS AT SEA WITH THE GRAND FLEET

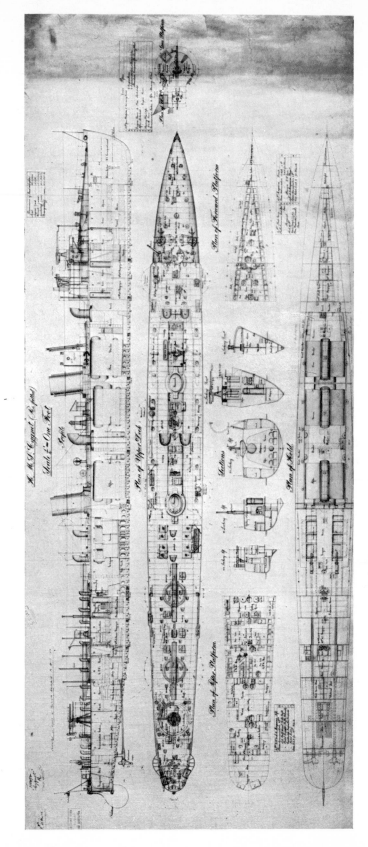

2. OFFICIAL DRAUGHT OF H.M.S. *CYGNET*, 1898

3A. SECOND CLASS TORPEDO-BOATS FITTING OUT AT
YARROW'S POPLAR YARD

3B. *ANGLER* FITTING OUT AT THE CHISWICK YARD OF
JOHN I. THORNYCROFT & CO. LTD.

4. *SPARROWHAWK* RUNNING HER TRIALS ''LIGHT'' IN 1895

5. *HORNET*, 1902

6. *HAVOCK* AS COMPLETED

7. *HAVOCK*, 1904. AFTER REBOILERING

8. *HASTY* AS COMPLETED WITH LOCOMOTIVE BOILERS

9. *CHARGER*, 1902. AFTER REBOILERING

10. *FERRET*, 1906

11. *BOXER*, 1913

12. *HAUGHTY*, 1898

13. *HUNTER*, 1905

14. *LIGHTNING*, 1909

15. *SALMON*, 1897

16. *CONFLICT*, 1913

17. *WIZARD*, 1912, REBOILERED WITH TWO FUNNELS

18. *FERVENT*, 1894, ON TRIAL, AS ORIGINALLY COMPLETED

19. *FERVENT*, 1907, AS COMPLETED FOR SERVICE

20. *STURGEON*, 1897

21. *OPOSSUM*, 1902

22. *SEAL*, 1914

23. *FOAM*, 1902

24. *BRAZEN*, 1909

25. *ALBATROSS*, 1908

26. *LEOPARD*, 1909

27. *STAR*, 1914

28. *BULLFINCH*, 1902

29. *RACEHORSE*, 1907

torpedo-boats of the mid-nineties could do better than this. The *Rattlesnake* and her sisters were reported as being satisfactory sea-boats but unsteady gun platforms and of flimsy construction, hence the building of the *Sharpshooter* class.

In 1893 there was an agitation about our deficiencies in torpedo-boats as the French were getting 23 or 24 knots out of their boats and Normand, the best French builder, hoped for 30 knots. The Admiralty refused to yield to this outcry, taking the view that torpedo-boats were the weapon of the weaker power. The true answer was to build vessels fast enough to catch and powerful enough to destroy foreign torpedo-boats, yet they should not be too large or too costly, so that large numbers could be built. The catchers had failed and so, in 1893, the first boat of a new type, the *Havock*, was launched by Yarrow, the design being that of Sir Alfred Yarrow and the Chief Constructor, Sir William White. In the same year, Yarrow also built the *Hornet* which had water-tube boilers and proved faster than the *Havock*.

These two boats were so successful that six more were ordered at once and another thirty shortly afterwards. Their designed speed was 27 knots, which was exceeded by some of the Thornycroft boats, but it was not very long before it was realized that their speed was insufficient. The *Forban*, built by Normand, and the *Sokol*, built by Yarrow for Russia, both reached 31 knots, so it was decided to build boats which could do 30 knots.

The *Havock* and *Hornet* took part in the naval manœuvres of 1894 and were regarded as sea-going torpedo-boats but it was said at the time that, as such, they were over-rated as a weapon of offence. The 1895 manœuvres were the first in which destroyers took part (apart from the *Havock* and *Hornet*) and after the 1896 manœuvres, *The Times* stated: "the game of the torpedo-boat is already up. The destroyer has beaten it out of the field."

Most of the early boats served with reduced torpedo armament to save top weight, but it must be realized that their function was a gunnery one and it was not until later that they became torpedo-boats also. Though they were able to remain at sea in weather which was too bad for contemporary torpedo-boats, they were wet and uncomfortable. Their turtle-back forecastles tended to make them bury their noses in the seas. It was said of the *Ardent*, when serving in the Mediterranean, that though life on board was hardly comfortable, it was endurable.

Though the early destroyers are termed the "27-knotters" few of them ever achieved this speed in service. Their trials were run "light" but when loaded, and in anything of a seaway, their speed dropped considerably. They

c

all suffered from vibration when running at high speeds, the worst period being at three-quarters of full speed. The high-powered engines in so flimsy a hull were expected to cause much vibration but it was reduced by Sir Alfred Yarrow's introduction of "balancing" the engines.

A steel screen was placed at the after end of the forecastle to prevent the decks being washed down at high speeds and canvas screens were fitted round the bridge. The conning tower was protected by half-inch plates but the hull plating was never as much as this, some parts being a quarter of an inch.

Surprise at night was not easy as the funnels were inclined to flame; even the most careful stoking could not eliminate this completely.

They carried three boats, a dinghy slung from davits and two Berthon collapsible boats. Anchors were catted just before the bridge. The accommodation was very cramped; usually the captain had a small cabin but the other officers lived in the wardroom.

In their early days, destroyers at home had black hulls, sometimes with a white rubbing strake and the turtle-back painted white. Abroad they had white hulls. For the annual manœuvres they often had numbers and funnel bands painted up.

In 1913 the 27-knotters were known as the "A" class and had their class letter painted on the bows and on one of the funnels. Before 1914 they were fitted with wireless; those which served in the First World War were (about 1916) painted grey with pendant numbers on the bows.

The draught given is the draught aft; the length is between perpendiculars.

HAVOCK, our first torpedo-boat destroyer.

Launched by Yarrow in 1893. 240 tons. 180 × 18·5 × 7·2 feet. 3,700 h.p. = 26–27 knots. Locomotive, then Yarrow boilers. One 12-pounder. Three 18-inch torpedo tubes. Complement 46.

The official trials were run on 28th October 1893 when she reached 26·78 knots, a world's record. She carried 57 tons of coal which gave her a radius of 3,000 miles at economical speed. The trials were so successful that six more boats were ordered at once and another thirty soon afterwards.

Certain modifications were necessary; she had rather too much top weight and so a torpedo tube was removed.

The *Havock*, with five other early destroyers (the *Hornet, Decoy, Daring, Ferret* and *Lynx*) carried a bow tube. This was proved to be a useless encumbrance as it was found that, at high speeds, the boat was liable to over-run the torpedo. Moreover, the tube was very much in the way and caused inconvenience in the living space forward. It also made the bridge extremely wet.

Originally, locomotive boilers were fitted, but in 1900 she was refitted with water-tube boilers which had, by then, proved their superiority over the earlier type.

The *Havock* served in Home waters and was sold in 1911. (*Plate Nos. 6 and 7*)

HORNET, launched by Yarrow in 1893. 240 tons. 180 × 18·5 × 7·5 feet. 3,700 h.p. = 27 knots. She made 27·6 knots on trial which was due to her Yarrow water-tube boilers. One 12-pounder. Three torpedo tubes. Complement 46.

She served in Home waters and was sold in 1909. (*Plate No. 5*)

CHARGER   HASTY   DASHER

Launched by Yarrow in 1894 (*Dasher* in 1895). 255–270 tons. 190 × 18·5 × 7·25 feet. Locomotive, then Thornycroft boilers. 3,700–3,800 h.p. (*Dasher* 3,180–3,800 h.p.) = 27 knots. One 12-pounder. Two torpedo tubes. Reboilered in 1900–01. Complement 53.

All served in Home waters. The *Charger* and *Dasher* were sold in 1911; the *Hasty* in 1912. (*Plate Nos. 8 and 9*)

	Launched	Disposal
BANSHEE	1894	Sold in 1912
CONTEST	1894	Sold in 1911
DRAGON	1894	Sold in 1912
FERRET	1893	Sold in 1911
LYNX	1894	Sold in 1912

All built by Laird. 290 tons. 210 × 19·5 × 9·4 feet. 4,400 h.p. = 27 knots. All had Normand boilers. One 12-pounder. Two torpedo tubes. (The *Ferret* and *Lynx* had bow tubes.) Complement 53. The *Banshee* and *Dragon*

served most of their time in the Mediterranean; the others served in Home
waters. Later in her career, the *Ferret* was experimentally fitted for boom
breaking. Her fore-bridge, gun and bow tube were removed and the turtle-
back forecastle was strengthened. (*Plate No.* 10)

	Launched	*Disposal*
ARDENT	1894	Sold in 1911
BOXER	1894	Lost in collision in the Channel in 1918
BRUISER	1895	Sold in 1914
DARING	1893	Sold in 1912
DECOY	1894	Lost in collision with the *Arun* off the Scillies in 1904

All built by Thornycroft. *Ardent, Boxer* and *Bruiser*, 265 tons. 200 ×
19 × 7 feet. *Daring* and *Decoy*, 260 tons. 185 × 19 × 7 feet. One 12-
pounder. Two torpedo tubes. (The *Daring* and *Decoy* had bow tubes.)
Complement 46–53. All had Thornycroft boilers. *Daring* and *Decoy* 4,200
h.p. = 27 knots. The others 4,300 h.p. = 27 knots. On trials the *Daring*
made 28·21 knots but the record for all the 27-knotters was held by the
Boxer with 29·08 knots.

All the early Thornycroft boats had sloping sterns and double rudders.
(*Plate No.* 11)

HARDY   HAUGHTY

Launched by Doxford in 1895. Sold in 1911 and 1912. 260 tons. 196 ×
19 × 7·5 feet. 4,200 h.p. = 26 knots. Yarrow boilers. One 12-pounder.
Two torpedo tubes. Complement 53. Both served in Home waters. (*Plate
No.* 12)

HANDY   HART   HUNTER

Launched by Fairfield in 1895. The *Hart* and *Hunter* were sold in 1912;
the *Handy* was on the sale list in 1914 and was sold at Hong Kong in 1915
or 1916. 275 tons. 194 × 19 × 7·5 feet. 4,000 h.p. = 27 knots. Thornycroft
boilers. One 12-pounder. Two torpedo tubes. Complement 53.

The *Handy* and *Hart* spent most of their time on the China station; the *Hunter* remained in Home waters. (*Plate No.* 13)

JANUS   LIGHTNING   PORCUPINE

Launched by Palmer's in 1895. The *Janus* was sold in 1912; the *Lightning* was mined off the East Coast in 1915; the *Porcupine* was sold in 1920. 275 tons. 200 × 19·5 × 8 feet. 3,900 h.p. = 27 knots. Reed boilers.

The *Janus* served on the China station most of her time and the others were in Home waters. *Lightning* is the oldest name connected with torpedo craft as it was the original name of T.B.1. (*Plate No.* 14)

ROCKET   SHARK   SURLY

Launched at Clydebank in 1894. The *Rocket* was sold in 1912; the *Shark* in 1911 and the *Surly* in 1920. 280 tons. 200 × 19·5 × 6·5 feet. 4,100 h.p. = 27 knots. Normand boilers. One 12-pounder. Two torpedo tubes. Complement 53.

All served in Home waters.

	Launched	*Disposal*
CONFLICT	1894	Sold in 1920
TEAZER	1895	Sold in 1912
WIZARD	1895	Sold in 1920
ZEBRA	1895	Sold in 1914

The first three were built by White, the *Zebra* by the Thames Ironworks, 320 tons (*Zebra* 310 tons). 200 × 20 × 8·2 feet. 4,500 h.p. = 27 knots. White-Forster boilers. One 12-pounder. Two torpedo tubes. Complement 53.

In 1910 the *Wizard* was reconstructed with only two funnels. She had in-turning screws and is believed to be the only destroyer to be so fitted. (*Plate Nos.* 16 *and* 17)

SALMON   SNAPPER

Launched by Earle's in 1895. Both were sold in 1911. 305 tons. 200 ×
19·5 × 7·7 feet. 3,600 h.p. = 27 knots. Yarrow boilers. One 12-pounder.
Two torpedo tubes. Complement 53.

Both served in Home waters. (*Plate No.* 15)

FERVENT   ZEPHYR

Launched by Hanna Donald in 1895 and sold in 1920. 275 tons. 200 ×
19 × 7·2 feet. 3,850 h.p. = 26–27 knots. Locomotive, then Reed boilers.
One 12-pounder. Two torpedo tubes. Complement 53.

Both served in Home waters. These boats originally had one funnel but
could not reach their contract speed so were reboiled with four funnels.
Even with water-tube boilers, the *Fervent* could not make her contract speed
of 27 knots and was accepted with a trial speed of 26·7 knots. Owing to these
troubles, these two boats did not leave their builders until 1901. (*Plate
Nos.* 18 *and* 19)

	Builder	*Launched*	*Disposal*
OPOSSUM	Hawthorn	1895	Sold in 1920
RANGER	Hawthorn	1895	Sold in 1920
SKATE	Vickers	1895	Sold in 1907
SPITFIRE	Elswick	1895	Sold in 1912
STARFISH	Vickers	1894	Sold in 1911
STURGEON	Vickers	1894	Sold in 1910
SUNFISH	Hawthorn	1895	Sold in 1920
SWORDFISH	Elswick	1895	Sold in 1910

265–295 tons. Dimensions varied slightly. 190–200 × 19·2 × 7·2–8·4
feet. 4,000 h.p. = 27 knots. The Hawthorn and Elswick boats had Yarrow
boilers; the Vickers boats had Blechynden. One 12-pounder. Two torpedo
tubes. Complement 53.

The *Skate* was the first destroyer to go to the shipbreakers, being only
twelve years old.

The *Skate*, *Starfish* and *Sturgeon* had their mast stepped before the
first funnel. (*Plate Nos.* 20 *and* 21)

THE THIRTY-KNOTTERS

THIS collection of slightly varying types were improvements on earlier designs and the speed was raised to thirty knots because of the increased speeds of foreign boats. The builders were allowed considerable latitude in the matter of design and the boats varied a good deal in detail and in appearance.

The best advertisement for these boats lay in the fact that they were worked very hard during the war years and though most of them were twenty years old by 1919, they remained efficient. This speaks well for their builders and for the dockyards which maintained them.

They were unable to keep up much of a speed in anything approaching bad weather, and their speeds dropped considerably. Moreover, they were very wet and uncomfortable. They had very cramped quarters though, as the boats increased in size, these conditions were slightly ameliorated. Their bridges were a little larger than in the earlier types.

Among the 30-knotters there were a few boats of new design notably the first turbine destroyers. It was not long before the turbine completely superseded the reciprocating engine.

One feature of these destroyers was their ability to keep afloat after receiving extensive damage. Their thin plating and light construction often made a horrifying picture after a collision but their watertight bulkheads stood and the boats were saved. They needed careful handling as their plates buckled easily and a bad alongside could not be disguised.

Many of these boats were completed with short funnels which were heightened soon afterwards.

When the system of class lettering was introduced in 1913 the 30-knotters were divided by appearance, the "B" class had four funnels, the "C" class three and the "D" class two.

The complement of all these boats was about 60.

EARNEST	LOCUST	QUAIL	SPRIGHTLY
EXPRESS	ORWELL	SEAL	THRASHER
GRIFFON	PANTHER	SPARROWHAWK	VIRAGO
LIVELY			WOLF

All were built by Cammell Laird between 1895 and 1901. The *Quail* was the first and the *Sprightly* the last to be launched. 355–400 tons. (The *Express* was 465 tons.) The average dimensions were 213 × 21·5 × 9·3 feet. The *Express* was 235 × 23·5 × 10·2 feet. 6,300 h.p. = 30 knots. One 12-pounder. Two torpedo tubes. All had Normand boilers. Complement 63.

The *Express* was a special boat and had large-sized boilers with 9,250 h.p. = 33 knots. In fact she never exceeded 31 knots; the freeboard of the midship portion was raised and sloped towards the stern.

The *Sparrowhawk* spent her time on the Pacific station and was wrecked in the mouth of the Yangtze in 1904. The *Virago* served on the China station; most of the others spent some years on the Mediterranean station between 1898 and 1905 and the *Quail* was in the West Indies for a few years. All served in the First World War and were sold between 1919 and 1921. (*Plate No.* 22)

	Launched	*Disposal*
ANGLER	1896	Sold in 1920
ARIEL	1897	Wrecked at Malta in 1907
COQUETTE	1898	Sunk by mine in 1915
CYGNET	1898	Sold in 1920
CYNTHIA	1898	Sold in 1920
DESPERATE	1895	Sold in 1920
FAME	1896	Sold in 1920
FOAM	1896	Sold in 1914
MALLARD	1896	Sold in 1920
STAG	1899	Sold in 1921

Built by Thornycroft, an improvement on the *Ardent* design. 310–335 tons. 208 × 19·6 × 7 feet. 5,700 h.p. = 30 knots. Thornycroft boilers. One 12-pounder. Two torpedo tubes. Complement 63.

These boats, later known as the "D" class, were constructed of a new high tensile steel to save weight. The first six had the sloping stern of previous

Thornycroft boats, but the last four had the standard type, showing the rudder above the water line.

The *Fame* served all her time on the China station. All the others served in the Mediterranean for varying periods but ended up in Home waters. (*Plate No.* 23)

	Launched	Disposal
BRAZEN	1896	Sold in 1919
ELECTRA	1898	Sold in 1920
KESTREL	1898	Sold in 1921
RECRUIT	1896	Sunk by mine in 1917
VULTURE	1898	Sold in 1919

Built at Clydebank. 345–350 tons. 214 × 20 × 8·3 feet. 5,800 h.p. = 30 knots. Normand boilers. One 12-pounder. Two torpedo tubes. Complement 63.

All served in Home waters. (*Plate No.* 24)

ALBATROSS

Launched by Thornycroft in 1898. 430 tons. 225·5 × 21·3 × 9 feet. 7,500 h.p. = 31·5 knots. Thornycroft boilers. One 12-pounder. Two torpedo tubes. Complement 69.

She was a very handsome boat, with a straight stern and single rudder. Up to 1913 she served in the Mediterranean and after that in Home waters. She was sold in 1920. (*Plate No.* 25)

	Launched	Disposal
AVON	1896	Sold in 1920
BITTERN	1897	Sunk in collision in 1918
LEOPARD	1897	Sold in 1919
OTTER	1896	Sold in 1915
VIXEN	1900	Sold in 1921

Built by Vickers at Barrow. 350–400 tons. 210 × 20 × 8·3 feet. 6,300 h.p. = 30 knots. Normand boilers, but the *Vixen* had Express boilers. One 12-pounder. Two torpedo tubes. Complement 63.

The *Otter* served on the China station all her time; the other four were always in Home waters. (*Plate No.* 26)

	Launched	Disposal
BAT	1896	Sold in 1919
CHAMOIS	1896	Foundered in 1904
CRANE	1896	Sold in 1919
FAWN	1897	Sold in 1919
FLIRT	1897	Sunk in action in 1916 in Dover Straits
FLYING FISH	1897	Sold in 1919
STAR	1896	Sold in 1919
WHITING	1896	Sold in 1919

Built by Palmer's S.B. Co. 360 tons. 215 × 20·75 × 9 feet. 5,900 h.p. = 30 knots. Reed boilers. One 12-pounder. Two torpedo tubes. Complement 63.

These boats had funnel caps and the steam pipes of the middle funnel were not in the centre line. Some of them served in the Mediterranean and later at Home. The *Whiting* spent her whole career on the China station. The *Star*, together with the *Ouse*, sank a U-boat in 1918. (*Plate No.* 27)

BULLFINCH   DOVE

Launched by Earle's S.B. Co. at Hull in 1898. They were sold in 1919 and 1920 respectively. 345 tons. 210 × 20·5 × 7·8 feet. 5,800 h.p. = 29 knots. Thornycroft boilers. One 12-pounder. Two torpedo tubes. Complement 63.

These two boats had flat-sided centre funnels and had conspicuous steam pipes. Both served in Home waters. (*Plate No.* 28)

	Launched	Disposal
CHEERFUL	1897	Sunk by mine in 1917
GREYHOUND	1900	Sold in 1919
MERMAID	1898	Sold in 1919
RACEHORSE	1900	Sold in 1920
ROEBUCK	1901	Broken up in 1919

Built by Hawthorn Leslie. 355–385 tons. 210 × 21 × 8 feet. 6,100 h.p. = 30 knots. Thornycroft boilers. One 12-pounder. Two torpedo tubes. Complement 63.

These boats had the usual Hawthorn funnel tops. All served in Home waters. (*Plate No. 29*)

VIPER

447 tons. 210 × 21 × 8·2 feet. One 12-pounder. Two torpedo tubes.

This boat was ordered from the Parsons Steam Turbine Co. who sub-contracted the hull to Hawthorn Leslie. She was the first destroyer in the Royal Navy to be fitted with turbines which were designed for 10,000 h.p. to give a speed of 31 knots. She had Yarrow boilers.

She ran her trials light (as was the usual custom at this time) and on her preliminary trials she reached 35·5 knots. On her official trials she did 33·75 knots, but these were affected by bad weather. In a later trial off Portsmouth she achieved 36·8 knots.

She was remarkably free from vibration and her fuel consumption was only 2·38 lb. per i.h.p. at 31 knots. She had eight screws on four shafts, of which the two outer ones were driven by the high pressure and the inner pair by the low pressure turbines. Each inner shaft had a turbine for going astern.

Unfortunately she had a very short life as she was lost in a fog off Alderney on 3rd August 1901, having been launched in 1899. (*Plate No. 30*)

VELOX

Launched 1902. Sunk by mine in 1915. 400 tons. 210 × 21 × 9 feet. One 12-pounder. Two torpedo tubes. Complement 63.

This boat was ordered from the Parsons Steam Turbine Co. who sub-contracted the hull to Hawthorn Leslie. Though in most respects the *Velox* belongs to the 30-knotter group, she was designed for 8,000 h.p. to give 27 knots. In addition to her turbines, she had small reciprocating engines for running at low speeds. She had Yarrow boilers. Later in her career she had four screws only, though as completed she had eight, on four shafts, two of which were driven by the reciprocating engines. Her whole career was spent at Portsmouth. (*Plate No. 31*)

	Launched	Disposal
FAIRY	1897	Sunk after ramming a U-boat in 1918
FALCON	1900	Lost in collision in 1918
GIPSY	1897	Sold in 1921
LEVEN	1898	Sold in 1920
OSPREY	1900	Sold in 1919
OSTRICH	1897	Sold in 1920

All built by Fairfield. 355–375 tons. 209 × 21 × 8 feet. 6,300 h.p. = 30 knots. Thornycroft boilers. One 12 pounder. Two torpedo tubes. Complement 63.

These boats had funnels of equal size. All served in Home waters. The *Fairy* sank a U-boat in 1918 and was herself lost as a result. The *Gipsy* sank a U-boat which had stranded on the Goodwins in 1917. The *Leven* sank a U-boat in 1918. (*Plate No.* 32)

	Launched	Disposal
LEE	1899	Wrecked near Blacksod Bay in 1909
SYLVIA	1897	Sold in 1919
VIOLET	1897	Sold in 1920

Built by Doxford and Sons at Sunderland. 350–365 tons. 210 × 21 × 9·7 feet. 6,300 h.p. = 30 knots. Thornycroft boilers. One 12-pounder. Two torpedo tubes. Complement 63.

All served in Home waters.

	Launched	Disposal
THORN	1900	Broken up in 1919
TIGER	1900	Sunk in collision with the *Berwick* in 1908
VIGILANT	1901	Sold in 1920

Built by John Brown & Co. at Clydebank as a speculation and were bought for the Royal Navy under a supplementary estimate of 1900–01.

380 tons. 218 × 20·7 × 9 feet. 6,400 h.p. = 30 knots. Normand boilers. One 12-pounder. Two torpedo tubes. Complement 63.

All served in Home waters.

TAKU

Launched by Schichau at Elbing for the Chinese Navy in 1898. She was captured at Taku in 1900 and served in the Royal Navy until 1916 when she was sold at Hong Kong. 305 tons. 194 × 21 × 5·8 feet. 6,000 h.p. = 32 knots. Schichau boilers. Six 3-pounders. Two 14-inch torpedo tubes. Complement 58. (*Plate No. 33*)

	Launched	Disposal
KANGAROO	1899	Sold in 1920
MYRMIDON	1900	Sunk by mine in 1917
PETEREL	1899	Sold in 1919
SPITEFUL	1898	Sold in 1920
SYREN	1901	Sold in 1920

Built by Palmer's. 370–400 tons. 215 × 20·8 × 9 feet. 6,200 h.p. = 30 knots. Reed boilers. One 12-pounder. Two torpedo tubes. Complement 63.

The *Kangaroo* and *Myrmidon* served for a time in the Mediterranean but the rest were always at Home. In 1904 the *Spiteful* had her boilers experimentally fitted to burn oil fuel and comparative trials were carried out with her sister, the *Peterel*. The dense clouds of smoke caused by the liquid fuel were a great drawback and serious experiments were discontinued for some years. These boats had a special form of funnel cap which was designed to prevent the seas entering the space between the funnel uptake and the outer casing. The last Palmer boat to have this device was the *Viking*.

Having four funnels, they were classified as "B" in the 1913 reclassification.

SUCCESS. 1901. Wrecked on Fife Ness in 1914.

Built by Doxford. 380 tons. 210 × 21 × 8·8 feet. 6,000 h.p. = 30 knots. Thornycroft boilers. Complement 63.

Served in Home waters. She was virtually a sister of the Palmer boats but without the distinctive funnel tops. (*Plate No.* 34)

COBRA. 1900. Broke her back in 1901.

Built by Armstrong Whitworth as a speculation though her turbines were ordered by the Admiralty. She was purchased in 1900 and was to have been altered after delivery. 400 tons. 223 × 20·5 × 8·5 feet. 11,500 h.p. = 31 knots. Parsons turbines and Yarrow boilers. One 12-pounder. Two torpedo tubes. She did 36·63 knots on trials.

The loss of the *Cobra* caused a reaction against turbines and high speeds generally. The cause of the disaster was never really determined; the break occurred about 150 feet from the bows, between the two after boilers. The loss of the boat, following only six weeks after that of the *Viper*, added to the loss of the cruiser *Serpent* in 1890, caused the Navy to object strongly to "snake" names. (*Plate No.* 35)

ARAB. 1901. Sold in 1919.

Built at Clydebank. 470 tons. 227·5 × 22·3 × 9·8 feet. 8,600 h.p. = 31 knots. Normand boilers. One 12-pounder. Two torpedo tubes. Complement 69. Served in Home waters. (*Plate No.* 36)

ALBACORE   BONETTA

Launched in 1908, as a speculation, by Palmer's and purchased in 1909 to replace the *Tiger* and *Gala* which had been lost. 440 tons. 215·5 × 21 × 7·5 feet. Turbines of 6,000 h.p. = 26·75 knots. Reed boilers. Oil fuel. Three 12-pounders. Two torpedo tubes.

Both served in Home waters and were sold in 1919 and 1920 respectively. (*Plate No.* 37)

THE "RIVER" CLASS

THE loss of the *Cobra* was one reason for the setting up of a "Committee on T.B.D." in the Admiralty towards the end of 1901. The result was the construction of boats with stouter hulls which meant that some sacrifice in speed had to be accepted.

The "River" class marked an entirely new departure in destroyer design. Their hull form made high speeds impossible but their radius of action was considerably increased for they carried 132 tons of coal, giving a radius of about 2,000 miles at economical speed. Only the *Eden* had turbines.

They had raised forecastles instead of the turtle-backs of earlier destroyers which made them more seaworthy and gave better living conditions. They were reliable boats, and though their speed was low they lost little in a seaway. They were designed for 26 knots, chiefly because of the conditions of trial which now had to be made with bunkers full and fully armed and equipped. It was pointed out at the time that destroyers built for the Japanese by Yarrow and Thornycroft were faster and able to remain at sea in bad weather during the Russo-Japanese War. However, the "Rivers" were probably as fast as the 30-knotters in a seaway.

As completed, they carried one 12-pounder and five 6-pounders, as their predecessors had done, but in 1907–08 they were given three additional 12-pounders. The earlier boats had sponsons at the break of the forecastle. For the first time, all officers had cabins. They carried a whaler and a dinghy on davits as well as a Berthon collapsible boat. Complement 70 in all.

The first batch of ten boats was ordered under the 1901–02 estimates. Each builder produced a class distinctive in appearance.

	Launched	*Disposal*
GALA	1905	Lost in collision with the *Attentive* in 1908
GARRY	1905	Sold in 1919
RIBBLE	1904	Sold in 1920
TEVIOT	1903	Sold in 1919
USK	1903	Sold in 1920
WELLAND	1904	Sold in 1920

Built by Yarrow. 590–605 tons. 225 × 23·5 × 10 feet. 7,500 h.p. = 26 knots. Yarrow boilers. One 12-pounder (later four 12-pounders). Two torpedo tubes.

The *Garry* had an improved form of hull which gave her a slightly greater speed. The *Gala* and *Garry* were different from the others as they mounted the guns abreast the bridge on the forecastle deck while the rest of the class mounted them in sponsons and had the hull cut away to allow of ahead fire. In addition, these two boats carried their anchors stowed flat on the forecastle while the others had recessed anchor beds. The four funnels were paired more widely than in the Palmer boats.

The *Garry* served at Home and in the Mediterranean. In 1914 she sank a U-boat off the Hoxa entrance to Scapa Flow.

The *Ribble, Usk* and *Welland* went to China in 1911. After the capture of Tsing-tao they went to the Dardanelles and remained in the Mediterranean for the rest of the war. The *Teviot* served in Home waters. (*Plate No.* 38)

	Launched	*Disposal*
CHERWELL	1903	Sold in 1919
DEE	1903	Sold in 1919
ERNE	1903	Wrecked in 1915 off Rattray Head
ETTRICK	1903	Sold in 1919
EXE	1903	Sold in 1920
ROTHER	1904	Sold in 1919
SWALE	1905	Sold in 1919
URE	1904	Sold in 1919
WEAR	1905	Sold in 1919

Built by Palmer's. 550 tons. 225 × 23·5 × 10 feet. 7,000 h.p. = 26 knots. Reed boilers. One 12-pounder (later four 12-pounders). Two torpedo tubes.

These boats had the typical Palmer funnels but they were more closely paired and had raking tops. In the four later boats guns were mounted on the forecastle deck instead of in sponsons.

The *Rother* was an additional boat being purchased under a supplementary estimate.

The *Dee, Erne, Ettrick* and *Exe* went to China for their first commission.

30. *VIPER*, 1900

31. *VELOX*, 1913

32. *FALCON*, 1907

33. *TAKU*, 1904

34. *SUCCESS*, 1905

35. *COBRA*, 1901

36. *ARAB*, 1909

37. *BONETTA*, 1912

38. *GALA*, 1906

39. *CHERWELL*, 1919

40. *COLNE,* 1909

41. *MOY,* 1905

42. *DERWENT*, 1910

43. *NESS*, 1914

44. *TARTAR*, 1908

45. *MOHAWK*, 1914

46. *COSSACK*, 1911

47. *AFRIDI*, 1911

48. *GHURKA*, 1909

49. *SARACEN*, 1911

50. *AMAZON*, 1914

51. *NUBIAN*, 1909

52. *CRUSADER*, 1911

53. *MAORI*, 1910

54. *VIKING*, 1911

55. *ZULU*, 1911

56. *ZUBIAN*

57. *BULLDOG*, 1911.
THE PLATFORM ABOVE THE BRIDGE WAS ONLY TEMPORARY

58. *RACOON*, 1912. ROUND FUNNELS

59. *GOLDFINCH*, 1911

60. *HIND*, 1914

61. *OAK*, 1913

In August 1905, the *Dee* and *Exe* were caught in a typhoon and steamed through the centre without coming to harm.

The *Wear* was in the Mediterranean during the war but the rest of the class served at Home. (*Plate No. 39*)

	Launched	Disposal
CHELMER	1904	Sold in 1920
COLNE	1905	Sold in 1919
JED	1904	Sold in 1920
KENNET	1905	Sold in 1919

Built by Thornycroft. Their tall funnels made them unmistakable. 550 tons. 220 × 23·75 × 9·25 feet. 7,500 h.p. = 26 knots. Thornycroft boilers. One 12-pounder (later four 12-pounders). Two torpedo tubes. The first Thornycroft destroyers to be constructed of high tensile steel. The *Jed* and *Kennet* had sponsons.

All four spent most of their time abroad. They went to the Mediterranean in 1911 and to China in 1913, later returning to the Mediterranean. (*Plate No. 40*)

	Launched	Disposal
ARUN	1903	Sold in 1920
BLACKWATER	1903	Lost in collision in 1909
FOYLE	1903	Sunk by mine in 1917
ITCHEN	1903	Torpedoed in 1917
LIFFEY	1904	Sold in 1919
MOY	1904	Sold in 1919
OUSE	1905	Sold in 1919

Built by Cammell Laird. 550 tons. 220 × 23·75 × 9·5 feet. 7,000 h.p. = 26 knots. Normand boilers. One 12-pounder (later four 12-pounders). Two torpedo tubes. The first four had sponsons.

The *Arun* and *Itchen* served for a short time on the China station but later served, as did all the others, at Home. The *Ouse* assisted in the sinking of two U-boats in 1918. (*Plate No. 41*)

D

STOUR   TEST

Built by Cammell Laird in 1905 and purchased in 1909 to replace losses. Both were sold in 1919. 570 tons. 220 × 23·75 × 9·5 feet. 7,000 h.p. = 26 knots. Normand boilers. Four 12-pounders. Two torpedo tubes.

These boats carried 134 tons of coal and 66 tons of oil. They served in Home waters.

	Launched	*Disposal*
BOYNE	1904	Sold in 1919
DERWENT	1904	Sunk by mine in 1917
DOON	1904	Sold in 1919
EDEN	1903	Sunk in collision in 1916
KALE	1904	Sunk by mine in 1918
WAVENY	1903	Sold in 1920

Built by Hawthorn Leslie. They had the usual flush funnel tops. 540–555 tons. 220 × 23·5 × 10 feet. 7,000 h.p. = 26 knots. Yarrow boilers. One 12-pounder (later four 12-pounders). Two torpedo tubes.

The *Eden* had Parsons turbines. The *Derwent*, *Eden* and *Waveny* had sponsons. All served in Home waters. (*Plate No. 42*)

NESS   NITH

Built by White at Cowes in 1905. Sold in 1919. 555 tons. 224·5 × 23·8 × 9·5 feet. 7,000 h.p. = 26 knots. White-Forster boilers. One 12-pounder (later four 12-pounders). Two torpedo tubes.

Both served in Home waters. (*Plate No. 43*)

THE FIRST "TRIBALS"

THESE were first described as "ocean-going" destroyers but their small radius of action, 1,500 miles at economical speed, rendered them fit for coastal work only. For this reason they were employed in the Dover Patrol during the war. Moreover, in most of them the forecastle was too short to make them particularly good sea boats. It has been said that Lord Fisher built these boats with the idea that they should act as small cruisers in the Northern Approaches to the North Sea to prevent the escape of German commerce raiders.

They were all different and their designed speed of 33–34 knots made them something quite out of the ordinary, especially after the "Rivers" with their 26 knots. As the torpedo gunboats gradually increased from the 525 tons of the *Rattlesnake* to the 1,070 tons of the *Halcyon* class, so destroyers increased from about 300 tons of the early boats to 800–1,000 tons of the "Tribals". Thus, it was suggested in Brassey's Naval Annual for 1908, the "Tribals" were destroyers of destroyers and might well have been called torpedo gunboats!

All boats were different, as the designs were left to the builders. The designed speed of 33–34 knots was not regarded with universal favour owing to the loss of the *Cobra*, but some of them ran their trials in rough weather and proved that these fears were groundless. The very high speeds with which the "Tribals" were credited in textbooks of forty years ago were mostly exaggerations. The first group was ordered under the 1905–06 estimates.

All the four-funnellers except the *Tartar* had their foremost funnels heightened before the war. They had three screws and were oil fired but carried only 185 tons of oil. The early boats were given three 12-pounders only but in 1912–13 two more were mounted. Later boats carried two 4-inch. The complement was about 70. In certain boats a modified turtle-

back forecastle was revived. They were such interesting boats that each one
is dealt with separately.

TARTAR

Launched by Thornycroft in 1907. Sold in 1921. 870 tons. 270 × 26
× 9 feet. Three (later five) 12-pounders. Two torpedo tubes. 14,500 h.p. =
33 knots. Thornycroft boilers. On trials she did 35·67 knots. She was the
first destroyer to be built at Woolston. (*Plate No.* 44)

MOHAWK

Launched by White in 1907. Sold in 1919. 865 tons. 270 × 25 × 8·75
feet. Three (later five) 12-pounders. Two torpedo tubes. 14,500 h.p. =
33 knots. White-Forster boilers. She reached about 37 knots on trials. Her
semi-turtleback forecastle was rebuilt before the war. (*Plate No.* 45)

COSSACK

Launched by Cammell Laird in 1907. Sold in 1919. 885 tons. 270 ×
26 × 9·2 feet. Three (later five) 12-pounders. Two torpedo tubes. 14,000
h.p. = 33 knots. Yarrow boilers. She was very successful and a fine sea boat.
(*Plate No.* 46)

AFRIDI

Launched by Armstrong Whitworth at Elswick in 1907. 872 tons.
250 × 25 × 7·8 feet. Three (later five) 12-pounders. During the war she
was re-armed with 4·7-inch guns. Two torpedo tubes. 14,250 h.p. = 33
knots. Yarrow boilers. She was at the sinking of a U-boat in 1916 and was
sold in 1919. There is a story that she was bought by a speculator and
hawked about for some years before being broken up. (*Plate No.* 47)

GHURKA

Launched by Hawthorn Leslie in 1907. Sunk by mine in 1917. 880 tons.
255 × 25·7 × 10 feet. Three (later five) 12-pounders. Two torpedo tubes.

14,250 h.p. = 34 knots. Yarrow boilers. She was at the sinking of a U-boat in 1915. (*Plate No. 48*)

SARACEN

Launched by White in 1908. Sold in 1919. 980 tons. 272 × 26 × 9·8 feet. Two 4-inch. Two torpedo tubes. 15,500 h.p. = 33 knots. White-Forster boilers. (*Plate No. 49*)

AMAZON

Launched by Thornycroft in 1908. Sold in 1919. 970 tons. 280 × 26·5 × 9·8 feet. Two 4-inch. Two torpedo tubes. 15,500 h.p. = 33 knots. Thornycroft boilers. (*Plate No. 50*)

NUBIAN

Launched by Thornycroft in 1909. 1,062 tons. 280 × 26·5 × 9·3 feet. Two 4-inch. Two torpedo tubes. 15,500 h.p. = 33 knots. Thornycroft boilers. 34·88 knots on trial. She was damaged by a torpedo in the action of 27th October 1916 and the wreck drifted ashore near the South Foreland. She was salved and, in 1917, the bow of the *Zulu* was joined to her, the resulting composite boat being named *Zubian*. (*Plate No. 51*)

CRUSADER

Launched by White in 1909. Sold in 1920. 1,045 tons. 285 × 26 × 9.8 feet. Two 4-inch. Two torpedo tubes. 15,500 h.p. = 33 knots. White-Forster boilers. (*Plate No. 52*)

MAORI

Launched by Denny in 1909. Sunk by mine in 1915. 1,035 tons. 280 × 27 × 9 feet. Two 4-inch. Two torpedo tubes. 15,500 h.p. = 33 knots. Yarrow boilers. At the sinking of a U-boat in 1915. (*Plate No. 53*)

VIKING

Launched by Palmer's in 1909. Sold in 1919. 1,090 tons. 280 × 27·3 × 9·75 feet. Two 4-inch. Two torpedo tubes. She was fitted with a 6-inch gun for a short time but this was removed later. 15,500 h.p. = 33 knots. Yarrow boilers. At the sinking of a U-boat in 1915.

The only six-funnelled ship in the Royal Navy. (*Plate No. 54*)

ZULU

Launched by Hawthorn Leslie in 1909. 1,027 tons, 280 × 27 × 9·3 feet. Two 4-inch. Two torpedo tubes. 15,500 h.p. = 34 knots. Yarrow boilers. In November 1916 she was mined and towed into port. Her bow portion was joined to the undamaged part of the *Nubian* in 1917 (*see Zubian*). (*Plate No. 55*)

ZUBIAN

In 1917 the bow of the *Zulu* and the stern of the *Nubian* were joined to make a new ship of 1,050 tons. Her approximate dimensions were: 288 × 27 × 9 feet. 15,500 h.p. = 33 knots. Yarrow boilers. Two 4-inch. Two torpedo tubes. The place where the two portions were joined was between the 3rd and 4th funnels so that she had three of the *Zulu*'s funnels and one of the *Nubian*'s. The fuel capacity was increased during the reconstruction. She sank a U-boat in 1918 and was sold in 1919. (*Plate No. 56*)

THE *BEAGLE* OR "G" CLASS

SIXTEEN boats were provided for in the 1908–09 programme and mark the first of a series of large classes, each mostly of the same design. The *Beagles* and several later classes were designed for 27 knots and were intended for service in the North Sea. These boats were too slow and under-gunned and were inferior to the contemporary German boats which were designed for 30 knots and mounted two 3·4-inch guns.

The *Beagles* were turbine and were the last coal-burning destroyers to be built for the Royal Navy. They mounted one of their torpedo tubes right aft, an unsatisfactory position, and later, some boats had it replaced by a small H.A. gun. This class was the first to carry 21-inch torpedoes.

The reversion to coal and the reduction of speed was considered at the time to be a retrograde step but the Admiralty may have been influenced by the fact that oil fuel was none too plentiful in this country. There was not yet a great deal of storage room and the Navy had very few tankers, only one of which, the *Petroleum*, was a large ship.

These boats were the first destroyers to have stockless anchors; they were, for their size, quite roomy and habitable. On completion, the "G" class boats were in the Home Fleet but on the reorganization of 1912 they went to the Mediterranean. Eight returned to England in 1915 but later returned to the Mediterranean. Late in the war, all these boats returned to Home waters.

In 1913–14 they were given funnel bands, at first white but later black or red. Their armament was one 4-inch on the forecastle and three 12-pounders. They mounted two torpedo tubes. Complement 96.

Some boats had three equal-sized round funnels; the others had two flat-sided funnels and the third one round.

	Launched	Disposal
BASILISK	1910	Sold in 1921
HARPY	1909	Sold in 1921

Built by White. 972–976 tons. 275 × 28 × 9 feet. 12,600 h.p. = 27 knots. White-Forster boilers.

The *Basilisk* sank a U-boat in 1918.

	Launched	Disposal
BEAGLE	1909	Sold in 1922
BULLDOG	1909	Sold in 1920
FOXHOUND	1909	Sold in 1920

Built by John Brown at Clydebank. 950–995 tons. 269 × 26·6 × 9·2 feet. 12,500 h.p. = 27 knots. Yarrow boilers. (*Plate No. 57*)

NAUTILUS (later GRAMPUS). 1910. Sold in 1920.

Built by the Thames Ironworks. 975 tons. 267 × 28 × 9·2 feet. 12,000 h.p. = 27 knots. Yarrow boilers.
She was renamed in 1913 as the name was required for a submarine.

RATTLESNAKE. 1910. Sold in 1921.

Built by the London and Glasgow S.B. Co. 946 tons. 270 × 27·5 × 9·3 feet. 12,000 h.p. = 27 knots. Yarrow boilers.

SCOURGE. 1910. Sold in 1921.

Built by Hawthorn Leslie. 922 tons. 267 × 28 × 8·8 feet. 12,500 h.p. = 27 knots. Yarrow boilers.

	Launched	Disposal
GRASSHOPPER	1909	Sold in 1921
MOSQUITO	1910	Sold in 1920
SCORPION	1910	Sold in 1921

Built by Fairfield. 923–987 tons. 271 × 27·7 × 8·7 feet. 12,000 h.p. = 27 knots. Yarrow boilers.
These, and all subsequent "G" class boats, had funnels of equal size.

PINCHER. 1910. Wrecked in 1918.

Built by Denny. 975 tons. 272 × 28·5 × 8·7 feet. 12,750 h.p. = 27 knots. Yarrow boilers.

	Launched	Disposal
RACOON	1910	Wrecked in 1918 on the Irish Coast
RENARD	1909	Sold in 1921
WOLVERINE	1910	Lost in collision in 1917

Built by Cammell Laird. 918–986 tons. 266 × 28 × 8·7 feet. 12,500 h.p. = 27 knots. Yarrow boilers. (*Plate No. 58*)

SAVAGE. 1910. Sold in 1921.

Built by Thornycroft. 897 tons. 264 × 28 × 9 feet. 12,500 h.p. = 27 knots. Yarrow boilers.

THE *ACORN* OR "H" CLASS

THESE twenty boats were built under the 1909–10 estimates and were an advance on their predecessors in that they were oil burners (they carried 130 tons) and mounted two 4-inch guns. Their displacement was less than that of the *Beagles* owing to the replacement of coal by oil. They proved faster on trials; the *Redpole, Ruby, Martin* and *Minstrel* exceeded 29 knots.

All had Parsons turbines except the Clydebank boats which had the Brown Curtis type. Yarrow boilers were in all but the White boats which had White-Forster.

The armament was two 4-inch and two 12-pounders with two torpedo tubes. All boats of this class were practically identical and had red funnel bands for distinguishing purposes. They constituted the 2nd Flotilla until 1915–16 when most of them went to the Mediterranean. The *Minstrel* and *Nemesis* were lent to the Japanese Navy in 1917 and were renamed *Sendan* and *Kanran*.

Their dimensions were 240 × 25·5 × 8·6 feet. Their i.h.p. was 13,500, giving 27 knots. Complement 73.

All were sold in 1921 except the *Hope* and *Martin* which were sold at Malta in 1920. War losses are given below. (*Plate No. 59*)

ACORN   ALARM   BRISK

Launched at Clydebank in 1910. 760–780 tons.

CAMELEON   COMET   GOLDFINCH

Launched by Fairfield in 1910. 747 tons.
The *Comet* was torpedoed in 1918; the *Goldfinch* was wrecked off the
Orkneys in 1915.

FURY

Launched by Inglis in 1911. 760 tons.

HOPE

Launched by Swan Hunter in 1910. 745 tons.

LARNE   LYRA   MARTIN   MINSTREL

Launched by Thornycroft in 1910 (*Minstrel* in 1911). 730 tons.

NEMESIS   NEREIDE   NYMPHE

Launched by Hawthorn Leslie in 1910 (*Nymphe* in 1911). 740 tons.

REDPOLE   RIFLEMAN   RUBY

Launched by White in 1910. 720 tons.

SHELDRAKE   STAUNCH

Launched by Denny in 1911. 748 tons.
The *Staunch* was torpedoed in 1917.

THE *ACHERON* OR "I" CLASS

Six of these boats were built to builders' designs but the whole class was very similar in most respects to the *Acorns* except that they had two funnels instead of three. The foremost funnel was raised in most boats about 1917.

As it was known that German destroyers were designed for 30 knots or more, pressure was put on the Admiralty to increase the speed of our boats. In consequence, six boats were built to their builders' designs though in appearance they were identical with the Admiralty design.

The two Yarrow boats were designed for 28 knots but actually did over 30 on trials; they had an improved type of steam superheater. The two Thornycroft boats were designed for 29 knots and this was easily exceeded. Two boats were contracted for by Parsons Steam Turbine Company who sub-contracted the hulls to Hawthorn Leslie. They were the first destroyers to have geared turbines for cruising. All mounted two 4-inch guns, two 12-pounders and two torpedo tubes.

All boats except the *Hydra* (1912) were launched in 1911. They were identical in appearance and had red and white funnel bands. Complement 71.

The whole class served in the Home Fleet and most of them were present at Heligoland, the Dogger Bank and Jutland. Some of them served in the Mediterranean and Adriatic later in the war.

These boats handled very well and were excellent sea boats. An officer who served in one of them and also in an Admiralty "R" boat says that they were much more dry at sea than the "R" especially when setting course and the stern swung into the sea. His feeling was that the "I" was real pre-war Clyde-built stuff whereas the "R" was obviously a war-time product. (*Plate No.* 60)

ACHERON   ARIEL

Built by Thornycroft. 763–773 tons. 251·75 × 26·4 × 9·3 feet. 15,500 h.p. = 29 knots. Yarrow boilers.

Both were involved in the sinking of a U-boat in 1915; the *Ariel* sank another in 1916. She later became a minelayer and was sunk by a mine in 1918. The *Acheron* was sold in 1921.

ARCHER   ATTACK

Built by Yarrow. 775–785 tons. 240 × 25·6 × 9 feet. 16,000 h.p. = 28 knots. Yarrow boilers.
The *Archer* never had her fore funnel heightened.
The *Attack* was torpedoed in 1917 and the *Archer* was sold in 1921.

BADGER   BEAVER

Built by Parsons/Hawthorn Leslie. 799–810 tons. 240 × 25·9 × 9·8 feet. 16,500 h.p. = 30 knots. Yarrow boilers. Both were sold in 1921.

Standard boats
750–775 tons. 240 × 25·75 × 9·3 feet. 13,500 h.p. = 27 knots. All had Yarrow boilers except the White boats which had White-Forster.

DEFENDER   DRUID

Built by Denny. Both were sold in 1921.

FERRET   FORESTER

Built by White. Both were sold in 1921. The *Ferret* was converted into a minelayer about 1918.

GOSHAWK

Built by Beardmore. Sold in 1921.

HIND   HORNET   HYDRA

Built at Clydebank. All sold in 1921.

JACKAL   TIGRESS

Built by Hawthorn Leslie. Sold, the *Jackal* in 1920 and the *Tigress* in 1921.

LAPWING   LIZARD

Built by Cammell Laird. Both sold in 1921.

PHOENIX

Built by Vickers. Torpedoed in 1918.

SANDFLY

Built by Swan Hunter. She became a minelayer in 1918 and was sold in 1921.

SPECIAL "I" CLASS

SIR ALFRED YARROW maintained that it was possible to build strong, seaworthy destroyers with a speed of 32 knots, and eventually a contract for three such boats was placed with his firm.

They were a little larger than the *Acheron* class and carried the same armament, but they were distinctive in appearance and were much faster. They all exceeded their contract speed, the *Lurcher* making over 34 knots.

FIREDRAKE   LURCHER   OAK

Launched by Yarrow in 1912. 765 tons. 225 × 25·6 × 10 feet. 20,000 h.p. = 32 knots. Yarrow boilers. Two 4-inch. Two 12-pounders. Two torpedo tubes. Complement 71.

Both the *Firedrake* and the *Lurcher* served at Harwich during the war and were fitted with long-range wireless for communicating with submarines in the Heligoland Bight. They had tall mainmasts. The *Firedrake* captured a U-boat in 1916 and sank another in 1917.

The *Oak* was tender to the Fleet Flagship of the Grand Fleet all through the war and had the distinction of having had the same commanding officer all her career. All three were sold in 1921–22. (*Plate No. 61*)

THE *ACASTA* OR "K" CLASS

THIS class consisted of twelve standard boats and eight special boats.

The standard boats were rather similar in appearance to the *Acorn* class but they had three 4-inch guns and had a designed speed of 29 knots. Five boats were built by Thornycroft and had a designed speed of 31 knots (*Hardy*, 32 knots). They were somewhat different in appearance from the standard boats.

The *Garland* was built by Parsons/Laird and was designed for 30 knots. She was framed on the Isherwood system but in appearance she was very similar to the standard boats.

The Fairfield-built *Fortune* was unique in appearance and seems to have been a "try out" for the three-funnelled "L" class. She had a clipper bow. Similarly, the *Ardent*, built by Denny, was perhaps a "try out" for the two-funnelled "L" class. These two boats were quite different from the rest of the class.

Parsons turbines were in all except the Clydebank boats which had Brown Curtis; all had Yarrow boilers. In the later stages of the war most of the survivors were fitted for special anti-submarine duties and their armament was altered. All were launched in 1912 or 1913. Complement 75.

On completion, the "K" class became the 4th Flotilla and though their base was changed from time to time, they remained the 4th until November 1918. All except the *Cockatrice*, *Paragon*, *Victor* and *Lynx* were at Jutland where four of them were lost. The *Shark* was sunk by German destroyers while screening Rear-Admiral Hood's battle-cruisers; the *Ardent* and *Fortune* were sunk during the night action, while the *Sparrowhawk* was rammed, first by the *Broke* and then by the *Contest* during the night. The *Marksman* found her next morning and sank her by gunfire.

The *Acasta* was badly damaged and towed home by the *Nonsuch*; during the night action the *Spitfire* came into collision with the German battleship *Nassau* and was severely damaged.

Standard design

935 tons. 260 × 27 × 10·5 feet. Three 4-inch. Two torpedo tubes. 24,500 h.p. = 29 knots. Complement 74. (*Plate No.* 62)

ACASTA   ACHATES   AMBUSCADE

Built at Clydebank. All were sold in 1921.

CHRISTOPHER   COCKATRICE   CONTEST

Built by Hawthorn Leslie. The *Contest* was torpedoed in 1917; the others were sold in 1921.

LYNX   MIDGE   OWL

Built by the London and Glasgow S.B. Co. The *Midge* reached nearly 33 knots on trial. The *Lynx* was sunk by a mine in 1915; the others were sold in 1921.

SHARK   SPARROWHAWK   SPITFIRE

Built by Swan Hunter. The *Shark* and *Sparrowhawk* were sunk at Jutland; the *Spitfire* was sold in 1921.

Special boats

GARLAND

Contract awarded to Parsons; the hull was sub-contracted to Cammell Laird. Sold in 1921. 989 tons. 260 × 27 × 10 feet. 24,500 h.p. = 30 knots. She reached 31 knots on trials. She was framed on the Isherwood system and was very similar in appearance to the standard boats but had a cut-away stern.

HARDY

Built by Thornycroft. Sold in 1921. 898 tons. 263 × 26·5 × 8·5 feet. 21,000 h.p. = 32 knots.

PARAGON   PORPOISE   UNITY   VICTOR

Built by Thornycroft and were similar in appearance to the *Hardy*. The *Paragon* was sunk in action in 1917 in the Dover Straits; the *Porpoise* was sold to Brazil in 1920; the *Unity* was sold in 1922 and the *Victor* in 1923. 917–953 tons. 263 × 26·5 × 10 feet. 22,500 h.p. = 31 knots. (*Plate No.* 63)

ARDENT

Built by Denny. Sunk at Jutland in 1916. 981 tons. 260 × 28 × 9·8 feet. 24,500 h.p. = 29.5 knots. (*Plate No.* 64)

FORTUNE

Built by Fairfield. Sunk at Jutland in 1916. 1,000 tons. 260 × 27 × 10·5 feet. 24,500 h.p. = 30·5 knots. (*Plate No.* 65)

THE "L" CLASS

THESE were the last destroyers to be completed before the war and the first to be named under the new alphabetical system. Their original names were changed before launching and are given in parentheses. In 1915, two more boats were added under the Emergency programme.

There were two groups; the six White and Yarrow boats had two funnels and the remainder three. Double torpedo tubes were mounted for the first

62. *SHARK*, 1914

63. *VICTOR*, 1914

64. *ARDENT*, 1914

65. *FORTUNE*, 1914

66. *LIBERTY*, 1914

67. *LOUIS*, 1914

68. *MELAMPUS*, CLASS

69. *TERMAGANT*, 1916

70. *ARNO*, 1915

71. *MANSFIELD* ON HER TRIALS

72. *READY*, 1920

73. *TYRANT*, 1924

74. *MURRAY*, 1919

75. *ORPHEUS*, 1920

76. *ROB ROY*, 1919

77. *SKATE*, 1919

78. *ROSALIND*, 1924

79. *UNDINE*, 1920

80. *VALOROUS*, 1924

81. *VENETIA*, 1932

82. *WINCHELSEA*, 1942, AS A LONG-RANGE ESCORT

83. *WALPOLE*, 1931

84. *WESTMINSTER* AS A "WAIR"

85. *WOOLSTON*, 1921

86. *STRENUOUS*, 1919. 14″ TUBES FITTED

87. *SARDONYX*, 1942

88. *TURQUOISE*, 1925

89. *TOURMALINE*, 1920

90. *WIVERN*, 1923

91. *WANDERER*, 1937

92. *WISHART*, 1921

93. *AMAZON*, 1926

time. The *Leonidas* and *Laforey* were the first destroyers to have geared turbines.

The *Lance* is generally supposed to have fired the first shot of the war when she and the *Landrail* sank the German minelayer *Konigen Luise* on 5th August 1914.

The "L" Flotilla saw a great deal of active service and took part in most of the actions, large and small, in the North Sea, though only one division was at Jutland. For some years they formed the famous Harwich Force.

965–1,000 tons. 260 × 27·5 × 10·5 feet. 24,500 h.p. = 29 knots. Parsons turbines except for the *Laurel*, *Liberty*, *Lassoo* and *Lochinvar* which had Brown Curtis. All had Yarrow boilers except the White boats which had White-Forster. Complement 72–76.

	Launched	Disposal
LANDRAIL (*Hotspur*)	1914	Sold in 1921
LARK (*Haughty*)	1913	Sold in 1923
LAVEROCK (*Hereward*)	1913	Sold in 1921
LINNET (*Havock*)	1914	Sold in 1921

Built by Yarrow.

LAUREL (*Redgauntlet*)	1913	Sold in 1921
LIBERTY (*Rosalind*)	1913	Sold in 1921

Built by White. (*Plate No.* 66)

LAERTES (*Sarpedon*)	1913	Sold in 1921
LYSANDER (*Ulysses*)	1913	Sold in 1922

Built by Swan Hunter.

LAFOREY (*Florizel*)	1913	Sunk by mine in 1917
LAWFORD (*Ivanhoe*)	1913	Sold in 1922
LOUIS (*Talisman*)	1913	Wrecked at Suvla in 1915
LYDIARD (*Waverly*)	1914	Sold in 1921

Built by Fairfield.

E

	Launched	*Disposal*
LANCE (*Daring*)	1914	Sold in 1921
LOOKOUT (*Dragon*)	1914	Sold in 1922

Built by Thornycroft.

LASSOO (*Magic*)	1915	Sunk by mine in 1916
LENNOX (*Portia*)	1914	Sold in 1921
LLEWELLYN (*Picton*)	1913	Sold in 1922
LOCHINVAR	1915	Sold in 1921

Built by Beardmore.

LEGION (*Viola*)	1914	Sold in 1921
LOYAL (*Orlando*)	1913	Sold in 1921

Built by Denny.

LEONIDAS (*Rob Roy*)	1913	Sold in 1921
LUCIFER (*Rocket*)	1913	Sold in 1921

Built by Parsons/Hawthorn Leslie. These two boats were of 22,500 h.p.
Many of the flotilla served at Dover from time to time; the *Laforey*, *Lawford*, *Louis* and *Lydiard* went to the Dardanelles in 1915 for a while. The *Liberty* sank a U-boat in 1917. The *Lawford*, *Legion* and *Loyal* were converted into minelayers in 1917. (*Plate No 67*)

PURCHASED BOATS

Medea class

These four boats were building for Greece and taken over for the Royal Navy. They were very similar in design to our "M" class though they differed in appearance; their tall mainmasts greatly added to their appearance.

Talisman class

These four boats were building for the Turkish Navy and joined the Fleet in 1916. They were large and heavily armed and though they appeared to be very like the *Medea* class, they differed in detail.

Arno

This small boat was building at Ansaldo's yard at Genoa for the Portuguese Navy and was bought in 1915.

	Launched	Disposal
MEDEA (ex-*Kriti*)	1915	Sold in 1921
MEDUSA (ex-*Lesvos*)	1915	Sunk in collision in 1916

Built at Clydebank.

	Launched	Disposal
MELAMPUS (ex-*Chios*)	1914	Sold in 1921
MELPOMENE (ex-*Samos*)	1915	Sold in 1921

Built by Fairfield. 1,007–1,040 tons. 265 × 26·7 × 11 feet. 25,000 h.p. = 32 knots. Yarrow boilers. Brown Curtis turbines. Three 4-inch. Four torpedo tubes. Complement 79.

The *Melampus* sank a U-boat in 1917. (*Plate No.* 68)

TALISMAN TERMAGANT TRIDENT TURBULENT

Launched by Hawthorn in 1915. Sold in 1921 except the *Turbulent* which was sunk at Jutland in 1916. 1,098 tons. 300 × 28·6 × 9·5 feet. 25,000 h.p. = 34 knots. Yarrow boilers. Parsons turbines. Five 4-inch. Four torpedo tubes. Complement 100.

These boats were originally given the names *Napier*, *Narborough*, *Offa* and *Ogre* but were renamed before launching. (*Plate No.* 69)

ARNO (ex-*Liz*)

Launched by Ansaldo, Genoa, in 1914 and purchased from Portugal in 1915. She was employed in the Eastern Mediterranean and was lost in collision in 1918. 600 tons. 230 × 22 × 7 feet. 8,000 h.p. = 28–30 knots.

Thornycroft boilers. Four 3-inch. Three 18-inch torpedo tubes. Complement 70. (*Plate No. 70*)

THE "M" CLASS

UNDER the 1913–14 programme 13 boats and a leader (the *Marksman*) were ordered. These were the prototypes of the War Programme boats and the "R" class was almost the same.

The two Hawthorn Leslie boats were quite different to the others and were the last four-funnelled destroyers to be built for the Royal Navy. Seventeen boats were built by Yarrow (there was never a Yarrow "R" class), and these had two funnels. Six boats were built by Thornycroft (and later, five of the Thornycroft "R" class) and these had three tall funnels. Finally there were 85 Admiralty "M" class, all much the same, with three short funnels. The original "M" boats had even shorter funnels. The early "M's" had cruising turbines but in the Repeat "M's" these were omitted to assist early delivery.

In order to arrange these boats in digestible form, they have been classified by builders. Details were much the same for all: they were about 1,000 tons displacement and their dimensions were 265 × 26·7 × 10·8 feet. Their complement was 79. They were of 25,000 h.p. = 34 knots. All except the White boats (White-Forster) had Yarrow boilers. The Clydebank, Fairfield and Stephen boats had Brown Curtis turbines; the others had Parsons. They had three screws and carried nearly 300 tons of oil. None of these boats was kept in service after the war but were sold, mostly in 1921. They formed the backbone of the Grand Fleet Flotillas until about 1917 when the "R" class came along. It will be seen that the names began with the letters M, N, O and P.

Their radius of action at 15 knots varied between about 1,500 miles and 2,500 miles (Admiralty design).

MANSFIELD   MENTOR

Launched by Hawthorn Leslie in 1914. 1,055 tons. 265 × 27 × 10·75 feet. Complement 79. 27,000 h.p. = 35 knots. Yarrow boilers.

The *Mentor* was at the sinking of a U-boat in 1917. (*Plate No. 71*)

Thornycroft "M" class

	Launched	Disposal
MASTIFF	1914	Sold in 1921
METEOR	1914	Sold in 1921
PATRICIAN	1916	Presented to Canada in 1920
PATRIOT	1916	Presented to Canada in 1920
RAPID	1916	Sold in 1927
READY	1916	Sold in 1926

985–1,070 tons. 271 × 27·5 × 10·75 feet. Complement 78. 27,500 h.p. (*Mastiff* and *Meteor*, 26,500) = 35 knots. Yarrow boilers with superheaters. The last four had Brown Curtis turbines instead of Parsons. The *Mastiff* reached 37·5 knots on trials. The *Meteor* was at the sinking of a U-boat in 1917; she became a minelayer in 1918. The *Patriot* sank a U-boat in 1917. (*Plate No. 72*)

Yarrow "M" class

	Launched	Disposal
MANLY	1914	Sold in 1921
MINOS	1914	Sold in 1920
MIRANDA	1914	Sold in 1921
MOON	1915	Sold in 1921
MORNING STAR	1915	Sold in 1921
MOUNSEY	1915	Sold in 1921
MUSKETEER	1915	Sold in 1921
NERISSA	1916	Sold in 1921
RELENTLESS	1916	Sold in 1926
RIVAL	1916	Sold in 1926
SABRINA	1916	Sold in 1927
STRONGBOW	1916	Sunk in action in 1917, while defending her convoy
SURPRISE	1917	Sunk by mine in 1917
SYBILLE	1917	Sold in 1926
TRUCULENT	1917	Sold in 1927
TYRANT	1917	Sold in 1939
ULLESWATER	1917	Torpedoed in 1918

All but the first three had sloping sterns, having had 2 feet added to the stern to improve the length on the waterline for speed purposes. 879–923 tons. First 10 boats: 260 × 26 × 10·8 feet. Last 7 boats: 269 × 25·75 × 10 feet. Complement 79. 23,000 h.p. = 35–36 knots. Yarrow boilers. Brown Curtis turbines. The *Tyrant* had double rudders.

The *Mounsey* reached 39 knots on trials. The *Miranda* was at the sinking of a U-boat in 1917. (*Plate No.* 73)

Early Admiralty "M" class

MATCHLESS. Swan Hunter.

MILNE, MOORSOM, MORRIS. Clydebank.

MURRAY, MYNGS. Palmer.

All were launched in 1914 and sold in 1921. (*Plate No.* 74)

Admiralty "M" class
All were launched in 1915–16. Nearly all the surviving boats were sold in 1921. (*Plate No.* 75)

MAENAD	MYSTIC (ex-*Myrtle*)	NICATOR
MARVEL	NARWHAL	PETARD
		PEYTON

Built by Denny.

MAGIC (ex-*Marigold*)	MEDWAY (ex-*Redwing*)
MEDINA (ex-*Redmill*)	MORESBY (ex-*Marlion*)

Built by White. The *Moresby* sank a U-boat in 1918.

MAMELUKE	MONS	NARBOROUGH	PENN
MARNE	NAPIER	OSSORY	PEREGRINE

Built at Clydebank. The *Marne* was at the sinking of a U-boat in 1918. The *Narborough* was wrecked in 1918 off the Orkneys.

MANDATE	MISCHIEF	ONSLAUGHT	ORIANA
MANNERS	OBSERVER	ONSLOW	PHEASANT
MINDFUL	OFFA	ORCADIA	PHOEBE

Built by Fairfield. The *Onslow* was at the sinking of a U-boat in 1918. The *Pheasant* was mined in 1917.

| MARMION | MARY ROSE | NESSUS | PARTRIDGE |
| MARTIAL | MENACE | NESTOR | PASLEY |

Built by Swan Hunter. The *Marmion* was sunk in collision with the *Tirade* in 1917. The *Nessus* was sunk in collision in 1918. The *Nestor* was sunk at Jutland. The *Partridge* and *Mary Rose* were sunk in action in 1917 defending their convoy.

NEGRO	NORMAN	NORTH STAR	ORIOLE
NONSUCH	NORTHESK	NUGENT	OSIRIS
(ex-*Narcissus*)			

Built by Palmer. The *Negro* was sunk in collision with the *Hoste* in 1916. The *North Star* was sunk during the attack on Zeebrugge in 1918.

| MICHAEL | MINION | NEPEAN |
| MILBROOK | MUNSTER (ex-*Monitor*) | NEREUS |

Built by Thornycroft. The *Michael* sank a U-boat in 1918. The *Milbrook* was at the sinking of a U-boat in 1918.

| NIZAM | NOMAD | PRINCE |
| NOBLE (ex-*Nisus*) | NONPAREIL | PYLADES |

Built by Stephen. The *Nomad* was sunk at Jutland.

NORSEMAN	OPHELIA	ORESTES
OBERON	OPPORTUNE	ORFORD
OCTAVIA (ex-*Orix*)	ORACLE	ORPHEUS
OPAL		

Built by Doxford. The *Ophelia* sank a U-boat in 1918 and the *Oracle* sank one in 1917. The *Opal* was wrecked in 1918 on the Orkneys.

OBDURATE	PALADIN	PLUCKY
OBEDIENT	PARTHIAN	PORTIA

Built by Scott.

PELICAN   PELLEW

Built by Beardmore. The *Pellew* was sunk in action in 1917 defending her convoy.

PIGEON   PLOVER

Built by Hawthorn Leslie. The *Pigeon* was at the sinking of a U-boat in 1918.

THE "R" CLASS

THE Admiralty "R" class, of which 39 were built, were slightly improved editions of the "M's". They were fitted with geared turbines which proved efficient and economical. To make them more seaworthy, the forecastle was raised by a foot and the flare of the bows increased, but in appearance the only noticeable difference was that the after gun was mounted on a band-stand. They had raked stems.

Five boats were fitted with high mainmasts to carry the aerials of Poulsen wireless. After the war this was taken out of the *Skate* which was the only boat of the "R's" to serve in the Second World War. The others which had the high mainmasts were the *Satyr*, *Sharpshooter*, *Starfish* and *Stork*.

The "R" boats began to pass into service in 1916 and were all sent to the Grand Fleet or the Harwich Force. They were retained in the post-war fleet for some years, those which were fitted as A/S training destroyers remained a few years longer. Had they been efficiently maintained in reserve, they would have been invaluable in the early stages of the Second World War.

Their displacement was 1,036–1,096 tons. 265 × 26·75 × 11·75 feet. Complement 82. The designed speed was raised to 36 knots with 27,000 h.p. All had Yarrow boilers except the two White boats which had White-

Forster. The Doxford and Hawthorn Leslie boats and the *Satyr* and *Sharp-shooter* had Parsons turbines; the others had Brown Curtis. The oil fuel capacity was increased in the "R" class and also in earlier boats as they came in for long refits.

Admiralty "R" class

RADSTOCK	**SORCERESS**	**TORRID**
RAIDER	**TORRENT**	

Launched by Swan Hunter in 1916 (*Torrid* in 1917). The first three were sold in 1927, and the *Torrid* in 1937. The *Torrent* was sunk by a mine in 1917.

RECRUIT   REDOUBT

Launched by Doxford in 1916. The *Recruit* was mined in 1917 and the *Redoubt* was sold in 1921.

REDGAUNTLET   ROB ROY   ROCKET

Launched by Denny in 1916. All were sold in 1926. (*Plate No.* 76)

RESTLESS	**ROMOLA**	**SIMOOM**	**TARPON**
RIGOROUS	**ROWENA**	**SKATE**	**TELEMACHUS**

Built at Clydebank. The first five were launched in 1916 and the last three in 1917. The *Simoom* was sunk in action with German destroyers in 1917; the *Rigorous* and *Telemachus* were sold in 1926; the *Tarpon* in 1927, the *Romola* in 1930, the *Restless* in 1936, the *Rowena* in 1937 and the *Skate* in 1947.

The *Tarpon* and *Telemachus* were fitted as minelayers in 1918. (*Plate No.* 77)

SABLE   SETTER

Launched by White in 1916. The *Sable* was sold in 1927. The *Setter* was lost in collision with the *Sylph* in 1917.

SATYR   SHARPSHOOTER   TANCRED

Launched by Beardmore, the *Satyr* in 1916, the other two in 1917. They were sold in 1926, 1927 and 1928 respectively.

SALMON (later *Sable*)   SPRINGBOK   TENACIOUS
SKILFUL   SYLPH   TETRARCH

Launched by Harland and Wolff at Govan, the *Salmon* and *Sylph* in 1916, the rest in 1917. The *Skilful*, *Springbok* and *Sylph* were sold in 1926, the *Tenacious* in 1928, the *Tetrarch* in 1934 and the *Salmon* (which had been renamed *Sable* in 1933) in 1937.

SARPEDON   STORK   THRUSTER
STARFISH   THISBE

Launched by Hawthorn Leslie, the first three in 1916, the others in 1917. The *Sarpedon* was sold in 1926, the *Stork* in 1927, the *Starfish* in 1928 and the other two in 1937.

SCEPTRE   STURGEON   TORMENTOR   TORNADO

Launched by Stephen in 1917. The *Tornado* was sunk by a mine in 1917 the *Sceptre* and *Sturgeon* were sold in 1926 and the *Tormentor* in 1929.

TEMPEST

Launched by Fairfield in 1917. Sold in 1937.

THORNYCROFT "R" CLASS

THE five boats of this class were improvements on the Thornycroft "M" type but, apart from the after gun being on a bandstand, they were similar in appearance. They were designed for 27,000 h.p. = 35 knots but all exceeded this easily on trials, the *Teazer* making over 40 knots. They had Brown Curtis turbines. Their dimensions were: $274 \times 27 \cdot 3 \times 11$ feet.

Thornycroft "R" class

RADIANT   ROSALIND   TEAZER
RETRIEVER   TAURUS

The *Radiant* and *Rosalind* were launched in 1916; the others in 1917. The *Radiant* was sold to Siam in 1920. The others were sold, the *Rosalind* in 1926, *Retriever* in 1927, the *Taurus* in 1930 and the *Teazer* in 1931.

The *Retriever* was at the sinking of a U-boat in 1918. (*Plate No.* 78)

ADMIRALTY MODIFIED "R" CLASS

IN 1916 a further design was produced with the idea of having better sea-keeping qualities. The bridge was moved farther aft on an extended forecastle and the extra deck space taken up was saved by transposing Nos. 1 and 2 boiler rooms bringing the double boiler room next to the engines and combining Nos. 1 and 2 funnels. Only eleven of these boats were built; all were launched in 1917.

The 4-inch guns had an elevation of thirty degrees instead of the twenty degrees in earlier types. The *Urchin* and *Ursa* had Parsons turbines; the others had Brown Curtis. They were of 1,076–1,091 tons. 276 × 26·8 × 11·8 feet. Complement 82. 27,000 h.p. = 36 knots. Yarrow boilers except in the White boats which had White-Forster. Three 4-inch. Four torpedo tubes. (*Plate No.* 79)

TIRADE   URSULA

Built by Scott. The *Tirade* was at the sinking of a U-boat in 1917 and was sold in 1921. The *Ursula* was sold in 1929.

TOWER

Built by Swan Hunter. Sold in 1928.

ULSTER

Built by Beardmore. Sold in 1928.

UNDINE

Built by Fairfield. Sold in 1928.

TRENCHANT   TRISTRAM

Built by White. Sold in 1928 and 1921 respectively. These boats had distinctive ribbed funnels.

ULYSSES   UMPIRE

Built by Doxford. The *Ulysses* was sunk in collision in the Clyde in 1918. The *Umpire* was sold in 1930.

URCHIN   URSA

Built by Palmers. Sold in 1930 and 1926 respectively.

THE "V" AND "W" CLASSES

IN order to counter the new German destroyers which were understood to be large and heavily armed, a new type was designed for the Royal Navy.

The first five boats were originally classed as leaders but later they were disrated to half-leaders and finally they were just destroyers. They varied between 1,316 and 1,339 tons displacement whereas the "V" class which followed were 1,090 tons and the "W" class were 1,100 tons. Internally they were quite different as they had extra accommodation for flotilla staff.

The four 4-inch guns were mounted forward and aft in super-firing pairs and this arrangement was continued in most of the succeeding classes until destroyers reached finality with the *Daring* class ships.

The "V" class, as completed, had four torpedo tubes in two pairs but later these were replaced by two triple tubes. The "W" class were completed with triple mountings; the *Voyager* being so fitted is included in the "W" class.

During the Second World War, many of these boats were converted into long-range escorts, their foremost boiler room being used as extra oil fuel stowage which entailed the loss of the foremost funnel; the h.p. was reduced to 18,000 for 24·5 knots. Their torpedo tubes were removed and the fitting of radar and HF/DF considerably altered their appearance. In many cases the guns in "A" and "Y" positions were removed (forecastle and quarter-deck). Others were converted into anti-aircraft escorts known as "Wairs". Their torpedo tubes were taken out and they were given two twin 4-inch High Angle mountings fore and aft. Their original complement was 110 though this was increased later.

Dimensions: 300 × 29·5 × 11 feet. 27,000 h.p. = 34 knots. Yarrow boilers in all except the White boats which had White-Forster. In the "Wairs" and long-range escorts the displacement was reduced to 900 tons.

The "V" and "W" destroyers were the backbone of our running flotillas for ten years after the First World War. They were popular boats, easy to handle and comfortable to live in under peace conditions. The first four running destroyers to be fitted with Asdics were a division of the 6th Flotilla —the *Windsor*, *Wessex*, *Westminster* and *Westcott*—in the early 1920s.

"V" half-leaders

VALENTINE   VALHALLA

Launched by Cammell Laird in 1917. The *Valentine* was bombed, grounded and abandoned in the Schelde in 1940. The *Valhalla* was sold in 1931.

VALKYRIE (ex-*Malcolm*)   VALOROUS (ex-*Montrose*)

Launched by Denny in 1917. The *Valkyrie* was sold in 1936 and the *Valorous* was broken up in 1948. (*Plate No.* 80)

VAMPIRE

Launched by White in 1917. She was transferred to the R.A.N. in 1932 and in 1942 she was sunk by aircraft bombs east of Ceylon.

1,316–1,339 tons. 312 × 39·5 × 9 feet. Complement 115. 27,000 h.p. = 34 knots. Yarrow boilers (White-Forster in the *Vampire*). Four 4-inch. One 3-inch. Four (later six) torpedo tubes.

"V" class

VANCOUVER (later *Vimy*)   VANESSA   VANITY

Built by Beardmore. The *Vancouver* was renamed *Vimy* in 1928. She sank two U-boats in 1942–43. Broken up in 1948.
The *Vanessa* sank a U-boat in 1942 and was broken up in 1945.
The *Vanity* was broken up in 1948.

VECTIS   VORTIGERN

Built by White and had the typical ribbed funnels.
The *Vectis* was sold in 1936; the *Vortigern* was sunk by an E-boat in 1942.

VEGA   VELOX

Built by Doxford. They were sold in 1948 and 1946 respectively.

VENDETTA   VENETIA

Built by Fairfield. The *Vendetta* was transferred to the R.A.N. in 1932, the *Venetia* was sunk by a mine in 1939. (*Plate No.* 81)

VERDUN   VERSATILE   VERULAM

Built by Hawthorn Leslie. The first two were broken up in 1945 and 1946 respectively. The *Verulam* was sunk by a mine in 1919.

VESPER   VIDETTE

Built by Stephen. Both were broken up in 1946. The *Vidette* was concerned with the sinking of four U-boats in 1943–44.

VIMIERA   VIOLENT   VITTORIA

Built by Swan Hunter. The *Vimiera* was sunk by a mine in 1942; the *Violent* was sold in 1937; the *Vittoria* was torpedoed in 1919.

VIVACIOUS   VIVIEN

Built by Yarrow. They were broken up in 1946 and 1945 respectively.

VANOC   VANQUISHER

Built at Clydebank. The *Vanoc* sank two U-boats in 1941 and 1944 and was broken up in 1945. The *Vanquisher* sank a U-boat in 1945 and was broken up in 1946.

VEHEMENT   VENTUROUS

Built by Denny. The *Vehement* was sunk by a mine in 1918 and the *Venturous* was sold in 1936.

"W" class (Plate Nos. 82, 83 and 84).

VOYAGER

Built by Stephen. Though a "V" name, the *Voyager* was completed with triple tubes and is therefore classified as a "W". She was transferred to the R.A.N. in 1932 and sank a U-boat in 1940.

WAKEFUL   WATCHMAN

Built by Beardmore. The *Wakeful* was sunk by an E-boat in 1940. The *Watchman* sank a U-boat in 1945 and was broken up in the same year.

WALKER   WESTCOTT

Built by Denny. Both were broken up in 1945; the *Walker* sank two U-boats in 1941 and the *Westcott* sank one in 1942.

WALPOLE   WHITLEY

Built by Doxford. The *Walpole* was broken up in 1945; the *Whitley* was damaged by aircraft bombs and beached off the Belgian Coast in 1940. The *Whitley* was the first "Wair".

WALRUS   WOLFHOUND

Built by Fairfield. The *Walrus* was wrecked on the Yorkshire Coast in 1938; the *Wolfhound* was broken up in 1948.

WARWICK   WESSEX

Built by Hawthorn Leslie. The *Warwick* was sunk by a U-boat in 1944; the *Wessex* was sunk by aircraft bombs off Calais in 1940.

WATERHEN   WRYNECK

Built by Palmer's. The *Waterhen* was transferred to the R.A.N. in 1932 and was sunk by aircraft bombs off Sollum in 1941. The *Wryneck* was sunk by aircraft bombs in 1941 during the evacuation of Greece.

WESTMINSTER   WINDSOR

Built by Scott's. They were broken up in 1948 and 1946 respectively.

WHIRLWIND   WRESTLER

Built by Swan Hunter. The *Whirlwind* was sunk by a U-boat in 1940. The *Wrestler* sank two U-boats in 1940 and 1942. She was scrapped after mine damage in 1944.

WINCHELSEA   WINCHESTER

Built by White and had ribbed funnels. They were broken up in 1944 and 1946 respectively.

Thornycroft "V" and "W" classes

VICEROY   VISCOUNT   WOLSEY   WOOLSTON

1,120 tons. 309 × 30·6 × 11 feet. 30,000 h.p. = 35 knots. Thornycroft boilers.

94. *AMBUSCADE*, 1935

95. *ACHERON*, 1935

96. *ICARUS*, 1937. FUNNELS NOT SHORTENED

97. *HESPERUS*, 1940

98. *MATABELE*, 1939

99. *TARTAR*, 1944

100. *JAVELIN*, 1941

101. *KINGSTON*, AS COMPLETED

102. *LIVELY* WITH EIGHT 4·7″ GUNS

103. *MATCHLESS*, 1943

104. *PALADIN*, 1958.
LIMITED CONVERSION TO FRIGATE

105. *QUEENBOROUGH*, 1942

106. *RELENTLESS*. FULL CONVERSION TO FRIGATE, 1953

107. *SAUMAREZ, 1943*

108. *UNDINE*, 1943

109. *VERULAM*, 1945

110. *CAESAR*, 1945

111. *COCKADE*, 1958

112. *SOLEBAY*, 1945

113. *AGINCOURT*, 1957

114. *CROSSBOW* AS RADAR PICKET, 1959

115. *DELIGHT*, 1959. ONLY FIVE TORPEDO TUBES

116. *HAMBLEDON*, 1942

117. *BLACKMORE*, 1945

118. *BLEASDALE*, 1945

119. *BRISSENDEN*, 1946

120. *CHURCHILL*, 1942. WITH CLINKER SCREEN

121. *NEWARK*

122. *LEEDS*, 1942

123. *STANLEY*, 1941

124. *SWIFT*, 1911

The *Viceroy* sank a U-boat in 1945 and was broken up in 1946. The *Viscount* sank two U-boats in 1942 and 1943 and was broken up in 1945. The other two were broken up in 1948. (*Plate No.* 85)

The following units of the "V" and "W" classes were converted before and during the Second World War:

"Wairs" (*A.A. escorts*)

Valentine	*Valorous*	*Vanity*
Vega	*Verdun*	*Viceroy*
Vimiera	*Vivien*	*Westminster*
Whitley	*Winchester*	*Wolfhound*
Wolsey	*Woolston*	*Wryneck*

Long-range escorts

Vanessa	*Vanoc*	*Vanquisher*
Velox	*Versatile*	*Vesper*
Vidette	*Vimy*	*Viscount*
Walker	*Watchman*	*Westcott*
Winchelsea	*Wrestler*	

The *Vivacious* and *Vortigern* were also converted to A/S escorts but it is uncertain whether the conversion included the removal of the foremost funnel. Oddly enough, inquiries in three different departments in the Admiralty have been unsuccessful.

THE ADMIRALTY "S" CLASS

IN 1917, intelligence was received about the contemporary German torpedo craft which led us to suppose that most of them were more lightly armed than our own boats. This led to a revision of destroyer design and it was decided to build boats which were smaller, faster and less expensive and which could be built quickly. These were known as the Admiralty "S" class. They were really an improvement on the modified "R" class, but the sheer forward of the forecastle was increased by two feet and the after end

F

reduced by a foot. The sides of the forecastle deck were rounded off and they had larger bridges with curved fronts. To save weight they had various modifications including the loss of the ram bow.

As first completed it was intended that they should mount two 14-inch torpedo tubes, one on either side of the break of the forecastle, for use against enemy destroyers. These were only mounted in the earlier boats and were removed after the war.

They were successful boats and had exceedingly nice lines. They were designed for 36 knots but many of them exceeded this on trials. The few that survived to serve in the Second World War were rather over-loaded and the weather in the North Atlantic was rather too much for them.

Many of these boats served in the Mediterranean soon after the First World War and saw much service in the Aegean and Black Seas. About twenty of them were there until 1923, when they were relieved by larger destroyers. In 1927, a flotilla of eight went to China until 1932. The majority were in reserve, some serving in various jobs at the Home Ports, but mostly they formed the Maintenance Reserve at Rosyth where, in 1928, there were 33 "S" class boats of which only 14 were in nominal commission, the rest being paid off. Naturally, they deteriorated and most of them were scrapped before 1939, which seems a great pity for they would have been most useful in the early stages of the war.

There were seven Yarrow "S" and five Thornycroft "S" boats; those built by Yarrow were distinguished by their sloping sterns. They reached very high speeds. The Thornycroft boats were larger and stood higher out of the water.

A number of the class were used for various experimental and special duties; the *Stronghold* (1923) and the *Thanet* (1928) both had aircraft catapults fitted on their forecastles for a time and several boats were disarmed while serving as tenders to aircraft carriers, and so on. The *Shikari* was for some time employed as controlling vessel for the wireless controlled target ships *Agamemnon* and *Centurion*.

Admiralty "S". 905 tons. 265 × 26·75 × 11 feet. Complement 98. 27,000 h.p. = 36 knots. Three 4-inch. Four-21 inch torpedo tubes and two 14-inch.
Yarrow "S". 930 tons. 269·5 × 25·75 × 9 feet. 23,000 h.p. = 36 knots.
Thornycroft "S". 1,075 tons. 267 × 27·3 × 9 feet. 29,000 h.p. = 36 knots (over 38 knots on trials).
Yarrow boilers in all except the White boats which had White-Forster.

They had Brown Curtis turbines except the four Palmer boats and the *Tilbury* and *Tintagel* which had Parsons.

They were all launched in 1918–19 except the *Thracian* which was launched in 1920. (*Plate Nos. 86 and* 87)

Admiralty "S" class

SABRE	Broken up in 1946
SALADIN	Broken up in 1947
SARDONYX	Broken up in 1945

Built by Stephen.

SCIMITAR	A U-boat in 1941. Broken up in 1947
SCOTSMAN	Sold in 1937
SCOUT	Broken up in 1945
SCYTHE	Sold in 1931
SEA BEAR	Sold in 1930
SEAFIRE	Sold in 1936
SEARCHER	Sold in 1938
SEAWOLF	Sold in 1931
SIMOOM	Sold in 1930

Built at Clydebank.

SENATOR	Sold in 1936
SEPOY	Sold in 1932
SERAPH	Sold in 1934
SERAPIS	Sold in 1934
SERENE	Sold in 1936
SESAME	Sold in 1934

Built by Denny.

SHAMROCK	Sold in 1936
SHIKARI	Broken up in 1945
SUCCESS	Transferred to the R.A.N. in 1919

Built by Doxford.

SHARK	Sold in 1930
SPARROWHAWK	Sold in 1931
SPLENDID	Sold in 1930
SPORTIVE	Sold in 1936
STALWART	Transferred to the R.A.N. in 1919
TILBURY	Sold in 1931
TINTAGEL	Sold in 1932

Built by Swan Hunter.

SIKH	Sold in 1927
SIRDAR	Sold in 1934
SOMME	Sold in 1932
SPEAR	Sold in 1926
SPINDRIFT	Sold in 1936

Built by Fairfield.

STEADFAST	Sold in 1934
STERLING	Sold in 1932
STONEHENGE	Wrecked near Smyrna in 1920
STORMCLOUD	Sold in 1934

Built by Palmer's.

STRENUOUS	Sold in 1932
STRONGHOLD	Sunk in action in 1942
STURDY	Wrecked on Tiree in 1939
SWALLOW	Sold in 1936
SWORDSMAN	Transferred to the R.A.N. in 1919

Built by Scott's.

TACTICIAN	Sold in 1930
TARA	Sold in 1931
TASMANIA	Transferred to R.A.N. in 1919
TATTOO	Transferred to R.A.N. in 1919

Built by Beardmore.

TENEDOS	Sunk by aircraft at Colombo in 1942
THANET	Sunk in action with the Japanese in 1942
THRACIAN	Captured by the Japanese at Hong Kong in 1942. She was recaptured at Tokyo in 1945 and sold in 1947
TURBULENT	Sold in 1936

Built by Hawthorn Leslie.

TRIBUNE	Sold in 1931
TRINIDAD	Sold in 1932
TROJAN	Sold in 1936
TRUANT	Sold in 1931
TRUSTY	Sold in 1936

Built by White. Only the *Tribune* and *Trinidad* had ribbed funnels.

TOMAHAWK (ex-*Woodpecker*)	Sold in 1928
TORCH (ex-*Wayfarer*)	Sold in 1929
TUMULT	Sold in 1928
TURQUOISE	Sold in 1931
TUSCAN	Sold in 1932
TYRIAN	Sold in 1930
TRYPHON	Wrecked at Mudros in 1919. Salved, and the wreck was sold at Malta in 1920

Built by Yarrow. These were particularly handsome boats. (*Plate No.* 88)

SPEEDY	Sunk in collision in 1922 in the Sea of Marmora
TOBAGO	Sunk by mine in 1920
TORBAY	Presented to Canada in 1928
TOREADOR	Presented to Canada in 1928
TOURMALINE	Sold in 1931

Built by Thornycroft. (*Plate No.* 89)

MODIFIED "V" AND "W" CLASS

IN 1918 a new class was begun; 57 were ordered but only 16 were completed, the others being cancelled at the Armistice. The 4-inch guns of the original "V" and "W" classes were replaced by 4·7-inch and the boats were a little larger. All were launched in 1919 except the *Wild Swan* and *Venomous* which were launched in 1918. Seven of the Admiralty designed boats had very large fore funnels and small after ones, not a very pleasing arrangement; the other seven were very similar in appearance to the "W" class. The two Thornycroft boats were, as usual, a little larger than the others and one knot faster.

1,120 tons. 300 × 29·5 × 11 feet. Complement 127. Four 4·7-inch and six torpedo tubes. 27,000 h.p. = 34 knots. Yarrow boilers except in the White boats which had White-Forster. Brown Curtis turbines except in the *Whitehall* which had Parsons.

Thornycroft boats

1,140 tons. 300 × 30·6 × 11 feet. 30,000 h.p. = 35 knots. Thornycroft boilers and Brown Curtis turbines.

These boats served at Home and in the Mediterranean, one flotilla being temporarily attached to the China station in 1926–28. In 1931, a flotilla of eight joined the China station, returning in 1934.

In 1942–43, the *Vansittart, Venomous, Verity, Volunteer, Wanderer* and *Whitehall* were converted into Long-Range Escorts. As in the "V" and "W" classes, the foremost boiler room was taken out and additional oil tanks fitted in its place. The foremost funnel was removed and the speed was reduced. The rest of the class were considerably modified for escort work but retained their funnels and all boilers. Y gun was removed and, in some cases, A gun also came out. Only one set of torpedo tubes was left.

VETERAN

Built at Clydebank. Sunk by a U-boat in 1942.

WHITSHED   WILD SWAN

Built by Swan Hunter. The *Whitshed* sank a U-boat in 1940 and was broken up in 1948. The *Wild Swan* was sunk by aircraft in 1942 in the Western Approaches.

WITHERINGTON   WIVERN   WOLVERINE   WORCESTER

Built by White. The *Witherington* sank two U-boats, in 1940 and 1943, and was broken up in 1945. The *Wivern* was broken up in 1945. The *Wolverine* sank three U-boats in 1941 and 1942 and was broken up in 1945. The *Worcester* was broken up in 1946. The *Witherington* and *Wivern* had oval after funnels. (*Plate No.* 90)

VANSITTART

Built by Beardmore. Broken up in 1946.

VENOMOUS (ex-*Venom*)   VERITY

Built at Clydebank. Both were broken up in 1946.

VOLUNTEER

Built by Denny. She sank a U-boat in 1942 and was broken up in 1948.

WANDERER

Built by Fairfield. She sank five U-boats between 1941 and 1944 and was broken up in 1946. (*Plate No.* 91)

WHITEHALL

Built by Swan Hunter. She sank three-U boats in 1943 and 1944 and was broken up in 1945.

WREN

Built by Yarrow. Sunk by bombing off Aldeburgh in 1940.

WISHART　　　WITCH

Built by Thornycroft. The *Wishart* sank three U-boats between 1941 and 1944. Broken up in 1945. The *Witch* was broken up in 1946. (*Plate No.* 92)

THE WAR-TIME DESTROYERS

THE main features of the design of the pre-war and war-time destroyers were fine sea-keeping qualities, ensured by their large freeboard and high forecastles, good fuel capacity and habitability. The design was so satisfactory that no other type of warship required less alteration during the war years —a tribute to their designers and builders.

The main duties of destroyers, as proved during the war, turned out to be of a nature not fully appreciated in 1914. It had always been intended that they should form an important part of the main fleet offensively and defensively. They were intended to carry out torpedo attacks on large enemy vessels and, in fact, at Jutland a good proportion of the German losses were inflicted by torpedoes from destroyers. They not only accompanied the Battle Fleet and battle-cruisers, but also operated with the light cruisers ahead of the main fleet. During the battle-cruiser action at Jutland, both sides sent their destroyers in to attack and a fierce action ensued between them. It was during this action that the *Seydlitz* was torpedoed by the *Petard*. Similarly, during the main action, destroyers were heavily engaged.

It was also the duty of destroyer flotillas to screen the fleet from submarine and destroyer attack, while it might also fall to their lot to carry out other duties such as when, at the Battle of the Dogger Bank in 1915, Vice-Admiral Sir David Beatty called the *Attack* to transfer his flag from the damaged *Lion* to rejoin his squadron. Destroyers were employed to screen damaged ships and to rescue the crews of disabled and sinking ships.

In addition to fleet work, destroyers were employed on operations both on their own and with light cruisers, the outstanding examples being the Harwich Force and the Dover Patrol. They were also used for patrol work in coastal waters and escorting merchant vessels.

For anti-submarine work, destroyers were recognized as being eminently suitable on account of their high speed and manoeuvrability. Later in the war, they were fitted with mine and explosive submarine sweeps which could be towed at high speeds. They also towed kite balloons.

Another use for destroyers was as fast minelayers for laying mines in the path of a retreating enemy (as was done by the *Abdiel* after Jutland) or laying fields off enemy coasts. There were 29 fitted for this purpose before the Armistice but only a few of these formed the permanent 20th Flotilla. It was possible to re-convert these boats as destroyers in twenty-four hours. In December 1918, the 20th Flotilla consisted of the following boats: *Abdiel*, *Gabriel*, *Ferret*, *Legion*, *Prince*, *Sandfly*, *Tarpon*, *Telemachus*, *Vanoc*, *Vanquisher*, *Venturous* and *Vittoria*.

Ideally, two distinct types of destroyer were needed:
(a) Destroyers for work with the Grand Fleet, with extensive radius of action and a good torpedo armament.
(b) Destroyers for service with the Harwich Force and at Dover where high speed and good gun-power were essential and the torpedo armament was of less importance. In fact, smaller and shorter-range torpedoes would have been acceptable.

But as war conditions required rapid output, it was not possible to specialize in destroyer construction, the war designs being considered suitable for both kinds of service. It was not until 1917, when the Grand Fleet Flotillas had been catered for, that the smaller boats of the "S" class were laid down.

Early in the war, the *Badger* rammed a U-boat (U-19; she was not sunk) and the damage to the fore foot resulted in the fitting to all destroyers of a sharp, square, ram stem.

RECOMMENCEMENT OF DESTROYER BUILDING

FOR some years after the war no new destroyers were laid down. The needs of the fleet were supplied by the war-time boats but it was evident that a programme of replacement must soon be put in hand, and with this in view the 1924–25 estimates provided for two experimental boats, the *Amazon* and *Ambuscade*, to be built by the two firms best known for this type of craft, Thornycroft and Yarrow.

The contract speed was 37 knots and for the first time a special super-heated steam device was installed. Boilers from now onwards were the Admiralty three-drum type. The forecastle was rather longer in proportion than in former destroyers and special attention was paid to sea-keeping qualities and habitability.

The lessons learned from these two boats were incorporated into the Admiralty design for the "A" class, and series of flotillas of eight boats each was built annually, all to this design. Triple torpedo tubes were replaced by quadruple mountings and, in the "I" class, by quintuples which had been tried out in the *Glowworm*. The speed was reduced by two knots.

From 1931–32, all destroyers had high mainmasts which were removed about 1940. The war-time alterations in the "A" to "I" classes followed a fairly consistent pattern. In 1940, nearly all boats had their after set of tubes taken out and replaced by a 3-inch H.A. gun. During the years 1942–43 the majority were converted into A/S escorts, sacrificing some guns and director control for additional A/S gear. The second funnel was reduced in height by seven feet, and later the 3-inch gun was replaced by a 20-mm. H.A. General warning radar and HF/DF on a vertical pole were fitted. Further details will be found under each class.

AMAZON

Launched by Thornycroft in 1926. 1,350 tons. 312 × 31·5 × 9·2 feet. 39,500 h.p. = 37 knots. Thornycroft boilers. Brown Curtis turbines with Parsons for cruising. Four 4·7-inch. Six torpedo tubes. Original complement 138. Sank a U-boat in 1940. Broken up in 1948. (*Plate No.* 93)

AMBUSCADE

Launched by Yarrow in 1926. 1,170 tons. 307 × 31 × 8·25 feet. 33,000 h.p. = 37 knots. Yarrow boilers. Brown Curtis turbines with Parsons for cruising. Original complement 138. Four 4·7-inch. Six torpedo tubes. Broken up in 1947. (*Plate No.* 94)

The "A" class

ACASTA   ACHATES

Launched at Clydebank in 1929. The *Acasta* was sunk in action with the *Scharnhorst* and *Gneisenau* in 1940, and the *Achates* in 1942 in the Barents Sea.

ACHERON

Launched by Thornycroft in 1930. Mined in 1940. (*Plate No.* 95)

ACTIVE   ANTELOPE

Launched by Hawthorn Leslie in 1929. The *Active* sank three U-boats in 1942–43 and the *Antelope* sank two in 1940. Both were broken up in 1946.

ANTHONY   ARDENT

Launched by Scott's in 1929. The *Anthony* sank a U-boat in 1944 and was broken up in 1946. The *Ardent* was sunk in action with the *Scharnhorst* and *Gneisenau* in 1940.

ARROW

Launched by Vickers-Armstrong in 1929. She was stripped at Taranto in 1944.

The "A" class were of 1,350 tons. 312 × 32·5 × 8·5 feet. 34,000 h.p. = 35 knots. The *Acheron* had special 500 lb. pressure boilers (others had 300 lb.). Parsons turbines except in the *Acasta* and *Achates* which had Brown Curtis. Complement 138. In the *Arrow* and *Anthony*, the after torpedo tubes were put back later in the war. When the surviving boats were modified as A/S escorts in 1942–43, Y gun was removed and extra depth-charges were added. In the *Achates*, A gun was replaced by a hedgehog.

The "B" class

BASILISK   BEAGLE

Launched at Clydebank in 1930. The *Basilisk* was sunk by aircraft off Dunkirk in 1940. The *Beagle* sank a U-boat in 1944 and was broken up in 1946.

BLANCHE   BOADICEA

Launched by Hawthorn Leslie in 1930. The *Blanche* was sunk by a mine in 1939. The *Boadicea* was sunk by aircraft off Portland in 1944.

BOREAS   BRAZEN

Launched by Palmer's in 1930. The *Boreas* was transferred to the Greek Navy in 1944. The *Brazen* was sunk by aircraft off Dover in 1940.

BRILLIANT   BULLDOG

Launched by Swan Hunter in 1930. Both were broken up in 1946.

The "B" class were of 1,360 tons. Other details as for the "A" class. The *Basilisk* and *Beagle* had Brown Curtis turbines. Later in the war, the after torpedo tubes were put back in the *Brilliant*. The *Bulldog* had a hedgehog in the place of A gun and had a 2-pounder mounted forward in the eyes of the ship for engaging E-boats. The *Boreas* kept her director.

The "C" class

COMET   CRUSADER

Launched at Portsmouth Dockyard in 1931.

CRESCENT   CYGNET

Launched by Vickers-Armstrong in 1931.

Originally there were to have been eight destroyers in this class which were provided for in the 1929–30 estimates, but the Labour Government of the time, as a gesture to other nations, reduced the number to four. The *Comet* and *Crusader* were the first destroyers to be built in a Royal Dockyard. All four were transferred to Canada in 1937–38.

1,375 tons. 317·75 × 33 × 8·5 feet. 36,000 h.p. = 36 knots. Parsons turbines. Complement 145.

The "D" class

DEFENDER   DIAMOND

Launched by Vickers-Armstrong in 1932. Both were sunk by aircraft in 1941, the *Defender* off Sidi Barrani and the *Diamond* during the evacuation of Greece.

DARING   DECOY

Launched by Thornycroft in 1932. The *Daring* was sunk by a U-boat in 1940. The *Decoy* was transferred to Canada in 1943.

DAINTY   DELIGHT

Launched by Fairfield in 1932. The *Dainty* sank two U-boats in 1940 and was sunk by aircraft off Tobruk in 1941. The *Delight* was sunk by aircraft off Portland in 1940.

DIANA   DUCHESS

Launched by Palmer's in 1932. The *Diana* was transferred to Canada in 1940. The *Duchess* was sunk in collision in 1939.

The dimensions of the "D" class were the same as those of the "C" class. The 3-inch H.A. gun was replaced by two 2-pounders in 1936. In 1942–43, the only surviving boat, the *Decoy*, was modified as an A/S escort; Y gun was removed, extra depth-charges fitted, HF/DF mast stepped aft and the director replaced by surface warning radar.

The "E" class

ECHO   ECLIPSE

Launched by Denny in 1934. The *Echo* sank a U-boat in 1943 and was transferred to Greece in 1944. The *Eclipse* sank a U-boat in 1943 and was mined in the same year.

ESCAPADE   ESCORT

Launched by Scott's in 1934. The *Escapade* sank a U-boat in 1940 and was broken up in 1947. The *Escort* sank a U-boat in 1940 and was sunk by a U-boat in the same year.

ESK   EXPRESS

Launched by Swan Hunter in 1934. Both were fitted as minelayers (*see* class notes). The *Esk* was sunk by a mine in 1940. The *Express* was transferred to Canada in 1943.

ELECTRA   ENCOUNTER

Launched by Hawthorn Leslie in 1934. Both were sunk in action in the Java Sea in 1942.

The "E" class were of 1,375 tons and their details were almost the same as those of previous classes. The *Esk* and *Express* were fitted as minelayers on completion though normally they served as destroyers. They were the first destroyers to have tripods and these tripod mainmasts were fitted to eliminate shrouds which would interfere with the minelaying gear. Radar was fitted in 1941–42 and later they had HF/DF masts aft. The *Escapade* had a hedge-hog in place of A gun and Y gun was taken out to compensate for additional depth-charges carried aft. The surviving boats were classed as Escort destroyers in 1943 but an official list of 1944 gives them as still mounting their full armament.

The "F" class

FEARLESS   FORESIGHT

Launched by Cammell Laird in 1934. The *Fearless* sank two U-boats in 1940 and 1941 and was sunk by bombing in the Mediterranean in 1941. The *Foresight* sank a U-boat in 1941 and was torpedoed in 1942.

FOXHOUND   FORTUNE

Launched at Clydebank in 1934. The *Foxhound* sank two U-boats in 1939 and 1941. She was transferred to Canada in 1943. The *Fortune* sank a U-boat in 1939 and was also transferred to Canada in 1943.

FORESTER   FURY

Launched by White in 1934. The *Forester* sank four U-boats between 1939 and 1944 and was broken up in 1946. The *Fury* sank a U-boat in 1942; in 1944 she was damaged beyond repair by a mine.

FAME   FIREDRAKE

Launched by Vickers-Armstrong in 1934. The *Fame* sank three U-boats between 1942 and 1944. She was sold to Dominica in 1949. The *Firedrake* sank two U-boats in 1939 and 1940. She was torpedoed by a U-boat in 1942.

Details for the "F" class were the same as in previous classes. All the surviving boats were rated Escort destroyers in 1943 and most of them gave up Y gun and had extra depth-charges, HF/DF and their directors replaced by surface radar. For a time, in 1942–43, the *Foxhound* was fitted with radar control for her main armament. The *Fame* had a hedgehog in place of A gun but it had been removed by early 1945.

The "G" class

GALLANT   GRENADE

Launched by Stephen in 1935. The *Gallant* sank a U-boat in 1940; in 1941 she was damaged by a mine and towed to Malta where she was bombed and sunk. The *Grenade* was sunk by aircraft off Dunkirk in 1940.

GARLAND   GIPSY

Launched by Fairfield in 1935. The *Garland* was lent to the Polish Navy from 1940 to 1946 and was sold to Holland in 1947. The *Gipsy* was sunk by a mine in 1939.

GLOWWORM   GRAFTON

Launched by Thornycroft in 1935. The *Glowworm* was sunk in action while ramming the *Hipper* in 1940. The *Grafton* was torpedoed by an E-boat in 1940.

GREYHOUND   GRIFFIN

Launched by Vickers-Armstrong in 1935. The *Greyhound* sank two U-boats in 1940–41 and was sunk by aircraft during the Battle of Crete in 1941. The *Griffin* sank a U-boat in 1940 and in 1943 she was transferred to the Canadian Navy.

The "G" class were 1,335 tons. 312 × 33 × 8·5 feet. 34,000 h.p. = 36 knots. They had tripod mainmasts which were removed from the surviving units of the class (*Greyhound* and *Griffin*) in 1941–42. Later, the *Griffin* was modified as an A/S escort; A and Y guns were surrendered and a hedgehog mounted in the A position. The director was replaced by surface radar. In 1940, the after torpedo tubes were replaced by a 3-inch H.A. gun.

125. *BROKE*, ON HER TRIALS

126. *MARKSMAN*, 1919

127. *SAUMAREZ*, 1920

128. *BROKE*, 1934

The "H" class

HASTY   HAVOCK

Launched by Denny in 1936. The *Hasty* sank two U-boats, in 1940 and 1941. She was sunk by a U-boat in 1942. The *Havock* sank a U-boat in 1940. She grounded and became a total loss in the Mediterranean in 1942.

HEREWARD   HERO

Launched by Vickers-Armstrong in 1936. The *Hereward* sank a U-boat in 1940 and was sunk by aircraft off Crete in 1941. The *Hero* sank two U-boats in 1942 and was transferred to Canada in 1943.

HOSTILE   HOTSPUR

Launched by Scott's in 1936. The *Hostile* was sunk by a mine in 1940. The *Hotspur* sank two U-boats in 1940–41 and was sold to Dominica in 1948.

HUNTER   HYPERION

Launched by Swan Hunter in 1936. The *Hunter* was sunk at Narvik in 1940. The *Hyperion* sank a U-boat in 1940 and was sunk by a mine in the same year.

Except that their displacement was 1,340 tons, the "H" class were the same as previous classes. The *Hereward* and *Hero* had a new type of bridge which incorporated an armoured navigating position which was adopted in all later classes. The surviving boats were reclassified as Escort destroyers in 1943. In 1942–43, the *Hero* and *Hotspur* (the only surviving boats) were modified as A/S escorts which involved the removal of Y gun. In the *Hero*, B gun was replaced by a hedgehog, but in the *Hotspur* the hedgehog was mounted amidships in the after torpedo tube space.

The "I" class

ICARUS   ILEX

Launched at Clydebank in 1936 and 1937 respectively. The *Icarus* sank four U-boats between 1939 and 1945. The *Ilex* sank three U-boats between 1939 and 1943. Both were broken up in 1946. (*Plate No.* 96)

G

IMOGEN   IMPERIAL

Launched by Hawthorn Leslie in 1936. The *Imogen* sank two U-boats in 1939 and 1940. She was sunk after collision in 1940. The *Imperial* was damaged by bombing off Crete in 1941 and was sunk by our own forces.

IMPULSIVE   INTREPID

Launched by White in 1937 and 1936 respectively. The *Impulsive* sank a U-boat in 1942 and was broken up in 1946. The *Intrepid* was sunk by aircraft in Leros Harbour in 1943.

ISIS   IVANHOE

Launched by Yarrow in 1936 and 1937 respectively. The *Isis* sank a U-boat in 1943 and was sunk by a torpedo or mine in 1944. The *Ivanhoe* sank a U-boat in 1939 and was mined in 1940.

Similar to the "G" class except that they displaced 1,370 tons. All were fitted for minelaying. In 1943, the *Icarus* was modified as an A/S escort; A and Y guns were removed and a hedgehog mounted in the A position. The *Impulsive, Ilex* and *Isis* were not reclassified as Escorts but remained fleet destroyers with full main armament and director control.

Additional units of "H" class

HARVESTER (ex-*Handy*)   HURRICANE

Launched by Vickers-Armstrong in 1939. The *Harvester* sank two U-boats in 1940 and 1943 and was torpedoed in 1943. The *Hurricane* was torpedoed in 1943. The *Handy* was renamed *Harvester* in February 1940 as its name was liable to confusion with *Hardy*.

HAVANT   HAVELOCK

Launched by White in 1939. The *Havant* was sunk by aircraft at Dunkirk in 1940. The *Havelock* sank three U-boats in 1940, 1944 and 1945, and was broken up in 1946.

HESPERUS (ex-*Hearty*)   HIGHLANDER

Launched by Thornycroft in 1939. The *Hesperus* sank five U-boats in 1942–45 and the *Highlander* sank one in 1940. Both were broken up in 1946. The *Hearty* was renamed *Hesperus* in 1940 to avoid confusion with *Hardy*.

These boats were originally built for Brazil and were purchased in 1939. Their Brazilian names were: *Japura* (*Harvester*), *Jurua* (*Hurricane*), *Javary* (*Havant*), *Jutany* (*Havelock*), *Jaguaribe* (*Hesperus*), *Juruena* (*Highlander*).

Details were the same as for the "H" class except that their displacement was 1,400 tons. All were completed without Y gun and extra depth-charges were carried instead. In 1942–43, surviving boats were modified as A/S escorts; A gun replaced by a hedgehog, the director removed and other modifications as in earlier classes. (*Plate No.* 97)

Ex-Turkish boats

INCONSTANT   ITHURIEL

Launched by Vickers-Armstrong in 1940 and 1941 respectively. Taken over in 1942. Details as for the "I" class. The *Inconstant* sank two U-boats in 1942 and 1944 and was returned to Turkey in 1946. The *Ithuriel* sank a U-boat in 1942 and was broken up in 1945. Y gun was removed from these boats but apparently all torpedo tubes were retained. Their Turkish names were *Muavanet* and *Gayret*.

THE NEW "TRIBALS"

In 1936, two flotillas of sixteen destroyers were laid down under the 1935 and 1936 estimates. They were much larger than the "A" to "I" classes and emphasis was laid upon gun armament rather than torpedoes for they mounted eight 4·7-inch guns in twin mountings and only four torpedo tubes. They were of 1,870 tons with dimensions 355·5 × 36·5 × 9 feet. They had Parsons turbines of 34,000 h.p. giving 36·5 knots. Their complement was 190. All were launched in 1937. The German destroyers laid down in 1934–35 were armed with five 5-inch guns and, on paper at any rate, were superior to the British "A"–"H" classes. The same applied to the large Italian Scouts launched in 1928–29. The new "Tribals" were intended mainly for breaking up enemy flotillas by gun action. They were too large and too costly for fleet work.

They had long forecastles, which detracted somewhat from their appearance but apart from their rolling propensities they were excellent ships and did splendid work during the war. Only four survived.

In 1941–42, the third 4·7-inch mounting was replaced by twin 4-inch H.A. guns and radar control was fitted for the main armament. The mainmast was removed, the second funnel shortened and HF/DF fitted on a pole mast aft. Later, surviving boats had their tripods replaced by lattice masts. In her later days (1946) the *Eskimo* had her torpedo tubes replaced by a deck-house.

AFRIDI   COSSACK   ESKIMO   MASHONA

Built by Vickers-Armstrong. The *Afridi* was sunk by bombing off Norway in 1940; the *Cossack* was torpedoed in 1941; the *Eskimo* was broken up in 1949; the *Mashona* was sunk by aircraft in 1941 in the North Atlantic.

ASHANTI   BEDOUIN

Built by Denny. The *Ashanti* was broken up in 1949; the *Bedouin* was sunk by an aircraft torpedo in the Mediterranean in 1942.

GURKHA   MAORI

Built by Fairfield. The *Gurkha* was sunk by bombing off Stavanger in 1940; the *Maori* was sunk by aircraft at Malta in 1942.

MOHAWK   NUBIAN

Built by Thornycroft. The *Mohawk* was torpedoed in 1941; the *Nubian* was broken up in 1949.

MATABELE   PUNJABI

Built by Scott's. The *Matabele* was torpedoed in 1942; the *Punjabi* was sunk in collision with the *King George V* in 1942. (*Plate No.* 98)

SIKH   ZULU

Built by Stephen. The *Sikh* sank a U-boat in 1942 and was sunk by shore batteries at Tobruk in the same year. The *Zulu* sank a U-boat in 1942 and was sunk by aircraft in the Eastern Mediterranean in the same year.

SOMALI   TARTAR

Built by Swan Hunter. The *Somali* was torpedoed in 1942 and the *Tartar* was broken up in 1947. (*Plate No.* 99)

THE "J", "K" AND "N" CLASSES

Three flotillas of large destroyers were laid down between 1937 and 1939. No leaders were built but one of each flotilla was fitted as a leader and named appropriately. These were the *Jervis*, *Kelly* and *Napier*.

The design, which was closely followed by later boats built during the war (apart from armament) was a departure from the "A" to "I" classes, the principal innovation being the adoption of twin gun mountings and a single funnel instead of two. They were considerably heavier than earlier types but had the same speed. They had a marked sheer forward. The *Kashmir* was the first Thornycroft boat to be longitudinally framed.

They were of 1,760 tons. 348 × 35 × 9 feet. 40,000 h.p. = 36 knots. Six 4·7-inch guns and ten torpedo tubes.

In 1940–41, the after set of torpedo tubes was replaced by a 4-inch H.A. gun; the "N" class was completed thus. Later in the war, this gun was taken out in some cases and the tubes replaced. The *Javelin* and *Jervis* had their tripods replaced by lattice masts.

All the "J" class were launched in 1938. (*Plate No.* 100)

	Builder	Disposal
JACKAL	Clydebank	Sunk by aircraft in the Mediterranean in 1942
JAGUAR	Denny	Sunk by a U-boat in 1942

	Builder	Disposal
JANUS	Swan Hunter	Sunk by aircraft torpedo off Anzio in 1944
JAVELIN	Clydebank	Broken up in 1949
JERSEY	White	Sunk by a mine in 1941
JERVIS	Hawthorn Leslie	Broken up in 1948
JUNO (ex-*Jamaica*)	Fairfield	Sunk by aircraft in 1941 during the Battle of Crete
JUPITER	Yarrow	Torpedoed in 1942 (She had sunk a U-boat in 1942)

All the "K" class were launched in 1939. (*Plate No.* 101)

	Builder	Disposal
KANDAHAR	Denny	Sunk by a mine in 1941
KASHMIR	Thornycroft	Sunk by aircraft in 1941 off Crete
KELLY	Hawthorn Leslie	Sunk by aircraft in 1941 off Crete
KELVIN	Fairfield	Broken up in 1949
KHARTOUM	Swan Hunter	Wrecked by an explosion off Perim in 1940
KIMBERLEY	Thornycroft	Broken up in 1949
KINGSTON	White	Sank two U-boats in 1939 and 1940. Sunk by aircraft at Malta in 1942
KIPLING	Yarrow	Sank a U-boat in 1941. Sunk by aircraft in 1942 in the Eastern Mediterranean

	Builder	Launched	Disposal
NAPIER	Fairfield	1940	In the R.A.N. until 1945. Sold in 1955
NEPAL (ex-*Norseman*)	Thornycroft	1941	In the R.A.N. until 1945. Sold in 1955
NESTOR	Fairfield	1940	Sunk by aircraft while in the R.A.N. service in 1942 in the Mediterranean

	Builder	Launched	Disposal
NIZAM	Clydebank	1940	In the R.A.N. until 1945. Sold in 1955
NOBLE (ex-*Nerissa*)	Clydebank	1940	Manned by the Polish Navy until 1946. Broken up in 1956
NONPAREIL	Denny	1941	Transferred to the Dutch Navy in 1941
NORMAN	Thornycroft	1940	In the R.A.N. until 1945. Broken up in 1957

Of the twenty-four boats originally ordered, two were sold to the Dutch and thirteen were lost during the war. They were the first one-funnelled destroyers to be built for the Royal Navy; the *Fervent* and *Zephyr* of 1895 never entered the Service thus. The two-funnelled design was not repeated until the "Weapon" class.

THE "L" AND "M" CLASSES

The "L" class

Two flotillas ("L" and "M") were next built. They were fine-looking ships, thought by some to be the most handsome destroyers ever built. Except for the four earlier "L" class, they were notable for their large power-worked turrets and they reverted to two quadruple torpedo tubes. Their displacement was 1,920 tons. 354 × 37 × 10 feet. 48,000 h.p. = 36 knots. The *Larne* was renamed *Gurkha* as a compliment to the Gurkha regiments, the men of which surrendered a day's pay each to pay for a new ship after the last *Gurkha* had been lost in 1940. All were launched in 1940–41. (*Plate No.* 102)

The "L" boats were in two batches. The earlier four (*Gurkha, Lance, Legion* and *Lively*) were completed with eight 4·7-inch guns in twin shields but the later four had six 4·7-inch dual purpose guns in closed, power-worked turrets. They were completed with radar control for the main armament and with general warning radar. The after set of tubes was replaced by a 3-inch H.A. gun in 1941–42, but these were reinstated by 1944 in the *Lightning, Lookout* and *Loyal*.

	Builder	Disposal
GURKHA (ex-*Larne*)	Laird	Sank two U-boats in 1940 and 1941. Torpedoed in 1942
LAFOREY	Yarrow	Sank two U-boats in 1943 and 1944. Torpedoed in 1944
LANCE	Yarrow	Broken up in 1944. She had been badly damaged by bombing at Malta
LEGION	Denny	Sank a U-boat in 1941. Sunk by aircraft at Malta in 1942
LIGHTNING	Hawthorn Leslie	Torpedoed by an E-boat in 1942
LIVELY	Laird	Sunk by aircraft in the Mediterranean in 1942
LOOKOUT	Scott	Broken up in 1948
LOYAL	Scott	Broken up in 1947

The "M" class

These were virtually repeats of the later "L" class boats but were completed with a 3-inch H.A. gun in place of the after torpedo tubes. By 1944, the tubes had been put back in the *Marne* and *Matchless*. By 1944, also, a lattice mast had replaced the tripod in the *Mahratta, Marne, Matchless, Meteor* and *Milne*. (*Plate No.* 103)

	Builder	Disposal
MAHRATTA (ex-*Marksman*)	Scott	Renamed as a gesture to India. Torpedoed in 1944
MARNE	Vickers-Armstrong	Transferred to Turkey in 1959
MARTIN	Vickers-Armstrong	Torpedoed in 1942
MATCHLESS	Swan Hunter	Transferred to Turkey in 1959
METEOR	Stephen	Sank a U-boat in 1944. Transferred to Turkey in 1959
MILNE	Clydebank	Sank a U-boat in 1944. Transferred to Turkey in 1959
MUSKETEER	Fairfield	Broken up in 1956

	Builder	Disposal
MYRMIDON	Fairfield	Transferred to the Polish Navy as the Orkan and did not serve under her British name. She was torpedoed in 1943

INTERMEDIATE, OR "O" TO "R" CLASSES

The War Construction programme began the building of many new destroyers. They were reduced and cheaper editions of the "J.K.N." group and in order to expedite delivery they were armed with such guns and mountings as were readily available. Their displacement ranged from 1,540 to 1,700 tons with a speed of 34 knots from 40,000 h.p.

They were very successful and most of those which survived the war joined the post-war fleet. A number have been sold to Commonwealth navies and most of the remainder have been converted into frigates, either fully or partially. These boats were considered by some people to be under-gunned but the fact remains that they could nearly always use what guns they had, no matter what the weather might be. They were strongly built and reflect the greatest credit on the naval architects who designed them and the builders who built them.

Of the "O" to "P" classes, the *Obdurate, Obedient, Opportune* and *Orwell* were fitted for minelaying. They were completed with either three or four 4-inch guns and with four or eight torpedo tubes. In 1943–44 their tripods were replaced by lattice masts and those boats which had only four torpedo tubes had another quadruple mount fitted. In the *Petard*, the main armament was altered to four 4-inch guns in two twins in B and X positions.

The "Q" class onwards were armed with 4·7-inch guns in four single mountings, and eight torpedo tubes. This was retained in all but the *Quickmatch* in which the after tubes were removed.

In the "R" class, the accommodation plan was altered, both officers and men being accommodated fore and aft. In really bad weather this meant that those quartered forward were "watch and stop on!"

In 1943–44, the tripods were replaced by lattice foremasts in the *Racehorse, Rapid* and *Redoubt*. (*Plates No.* 104, 105 *and* 106)

	Builder	Launched	Disposal
OBDURATE	Denny	1942	Broken up in 1956
OBEDIENT	Denny	1942	
OFFA	Fairfield	1941	Sold to Pakistan in 1949
ONSLAUGHT (ex-*Pathfinder*)	Fairfield	1941	Sold to Pakistan in 1951
ONSLOW (ex-*Pakenham*)	Clydebank	1941	Sank a U-boat in 1942. Sold to Pakistan in 1949
OPPORTUNE	Thornycroft	1942	Converted to a frigate in 1955
ORIBI (ex-*Observer*)	Fairfield	1941	Sank a U-boat in 1943. Transferred to Turkey in 1946

(Named as a compliment to South Africa)

	Builder	Launched	Disposal
ORWELL	Fairfield	1942	Converted to a frigate in 1952
PAKENHAM (ex-*Onslow*)	Hawthorn Leslie	1941	Sank two U-boats in 1942 and 1943. Sunk after damage in action in 1943 off Sicily
PALADIN	Clydebank	1941	Sank two U-boats in 1943 and 1944. Converted to a frigate in 1954
PANTHER	Fairfield	1941	Sunk by aircraft in the Aegean in 1943
PARTRIDGE	Fairfield	1941	Torpedoed in 1942
PATHFINDER (ex-*Onslaught*)	Hawthorn Leslie	1941	Sank three U-boats in 1942–43. Broken up in 1946
PENN	Hawthorn Leslie	1941	Broken up in 1948
PETARD (ex-*Persistent*)	Vickers-Armstrong	1941	Sank three U-boats in 1942 and 1944. Converted to a frigate in 1955
PORCUPINE	Vickers-Armstrong	1941	Torpedoed in 1943 but the fore part was salved and towed home to become a landing craft base in 1944. Broken up in 1947
QUADRANT	Hawthorn Leslie	1942	Transferred to the R.A.N. in 1945
QUAIL	Hawthorn Leslie	1942	Mined in 1943 and sank while in tow in 1944

	Builder	*Launched*	*Disposal*
QUALITY	Swan Hunter	1941	Transferred to the R.A.N. in 1945
QUEENBOROUGH	Swan Hunter	1942	Transferred to the R.A.N. in 1945
QUENTIN	White	1941	Sank two U-boats in 1942. Sunk by aircraft torpedo in 1942 in the Western Mediterranean
QUIBERON	White	1942	Sank a U-boat in 1942. Transferred to the R.A.N. in 1945
QUICKMATCH	White	1942	Transferred to the R.A.N. in 1945
QUILLIAM	Hawthorn Leslie	1941	Sold to Holland in 1945
RACEHORSE	Clydebank	1942	Broken up in 1949
RAIDER	Cammell Laird	1942	Transferred to India in 1949
RAPID	Cammell Laird	1942	Converted to a frigate in 1953
REDOUBT	Clydebank	1942	Transferred to India in 1949
RELENTLESS	Clydebank	1942	Converted to a frigate in 1951
ROCKET	Scott	1942	Converted to a frigate in 1951
ROEBUCK	Scott	1942	Converted to a frigate in 1953
ROTHERHAM	Hawthorn Leslie	1942	Damaged by a mine in 1946 and subsequently sunk as not being worth repair

THE "S" TO "Z" CLASSES

The "S" to "Z" groups were officially known as a "utility" type in which essential war requirements took precedence over all other considerations. Their finish was below the standard required in peacetime and many fittings, considered necessary in the "J" class, were omitted.

The "S" class

1,796 tons. 362·75 × 35·7 × 10 feet. 40,000 h.p. = 34 knots. Complement 232.

The *Savage* was completed with a special armament of four 4·5-inch dual-purpose guns in one twin and two single mountings. The twin turret forward was a prototype for those later fitted in the "Battle" class.

The *Saumarez, Scourge, Serapis* and *Swift* were completed with lattice foremasts and later one was also fitted in the *Scorpion. (Plate No.* 107)

	Builder	Launched	Disposal
SAUMAREZ	Hawthorn Leslie	1942	Damaged by a mine in 1946 and subsequently sunk as not being worth repair
SAVAGE	Hawthorn Leslie	1942	
SCORPION (ex-*Sentinel*)	Cammell Laird	1942	Sold to Holland in 1945
SCOURGE	Cammell Laird	1942	Sold to Holland in 1945
SERAPIS	Scott	1943	Sold to Holland in 1945
SHARK	Scott	1943	Transferred to Norway in 1944
SUCCESS	White	1943	Transferred to Norway in 1943
SWIFT	White	1943	Sunk by a mine in 1944

The "T" class

1,710 tons. Other details as for "S" class.

The *Tumult* was completed with a temporary experimental torpedo armament comprising two single, fixed, tubes amidships, angled slightly outwards, instead of the forward quadruple mounting. The *Teazer, Tenacious, Termagant* and *Terpsichore* were completed with lattice foremasts which were also fitted later in the *Troubridge, Tumult* and *Tuscan.*

	Builder	Launched	Disposal
TEAZER	Cammell Laird	1943	Converted to a frigate in 1954
TENACIOUS	Cammell Laird	1943	Converted to a frigate in 1952
TERMAGANT	Denny	1943	Converted to a frigate in 1954
TERPSICHORE	Denny	1943	Converted to a frigate in 1954
TROUBRIDGE	Clydebank	1942	Sank a U-boat in 1944. Converted to a frigate in 1955
TUMULT	Clydebank	1942	Sank a U-boat in 1944. Converted to a frigate in 1954
TUSCAN	Swan Hunter	1942	Converted to a frigate in 1954
TYRIAN	Swan Hunter	1942	Converted to a frigate in 1954

The "U" class

This class, and all succeeding classes down to the "Z" class, had the same details as for the previous class. From this time onwards, the leaders were given names not beginning with the class letter. Only the *Grenville* and *Ulster* were completed with tripods and these were replaced by lattice masts in 1944–45. All units of this class were converted into frigates in 1953–54. (*Plate No.* 108)

	Builder	Launched
GRENVILLE	Swan Hunter	1942
ULSTER	Swan Hunter	1942
ULYSSES	Cammell Laird	1943
UNDAUNTED	Cammell Laird	1943
UNDINE	Thornycroft	1943
URANIA	Vickers-Armstrong	1943
URCHIN	Vickers-Armstrong	1943
URSA	Thornycroft	1943

The "V" class

All except the *Venus* were completed with lattice masts and this boat had one later. (*Plate No.* 109)

	Builder	Launched	Disposal
HARDY	Clydebank	1943	Torpedoed in 1944
VALENTINE (ex-*Kempenfelt*)	Clydebank	1943	Transferred to Canada in 1944
VENUS	Fairfield	1943	Converted to a frigate in 1952
VERULAM	Fairfield	1943	Converted to a frigate in 1952
VIGILANT	Swan Hunter	1942	Converted to a frigate in 1952
VIRAGO	Swan Hunter	1943	Converted to a frigate in 1952
VIXEN	White	1943	Transferred to Canada in 1944
VOLAGE	White	1943	Converted to a frigate in 1952

The "W" class

These were the last British destroyers completed with 4·7-inch L.A. main armament and they were the first entire class to be completed with lattice masts.

	Builder	Launched	Disposal
KEMPENFELT (ex-*Valentine*)	Clydebank	1943	Sold to Yugoslavia in 1957
WAGER	Clydebank	1943	Sold to Yugoslavia in 1957
WAKEFUL (ex-*Zebra*)	Denny	1943	Converted to a frigate in 1953
WESSEX (ex-*Zenith*)	Denny	1943	Sold to South Africa in 1950
WHELP	Hawthorn Leslie	1943	Sold to South Africa in 1952
WHIRLWIND	Hawthorn Leslie	1943	Converted to a frigate in 1953
WIZARD	Vickers-Armstrong	1943	Converted to a frigate in 1954
WRANGLER	Vickers-Armstrong	1943	Converted to a frigate in 1952

The "Z" class

This was the last class of the 48 almost identical war-time "utility" destroyers. The "Z" class differed from the others in having 4·5-inch dual purpose guns as their main armament.

	Builder	Launched	Disposal
MYNGS	Parsons/ Vickers	1943	Sold to Egypt in 1955
ZAMBESI	Cammell Laird	1943	Converted to a frigate in 1955
ZEALOUS	Cammell Laird	1944	Sold to Israel in 1955
ZEBRA (ex-*Wakeful*)	Denny	1944	Broken up in 1958
ZENITH (ex-*Wessex*)	Denny	1944	Sold to Egypt in 1955

	Builder	Launched	Disposal
ZEPHYR	Parsons/ Vickers	1943	Broken up in 1958
ZEST	Thornycroft	1943	Converted to a frigate in 1955
ZODIAC	Thornycroft	1944	Sold to Israel in 1955

THE "C" CLASSES

AFTER the "Z" class had been named, it was decided to go back and use earlier letters for ensuing classes but it was found, after a few names had been allotted, that the new destroyers were to be given power worked mountings and a new, large type of director. To compensate for this, one set of torpedo tubes was to be surrendered. These new destroyers were evidently to be an advance on the Intermediate type and so a fresh set of names was chosen.

Originally it was intended to build four flotillas of eight boats each, but as it turned out six of the Cr- group never commissioned in the Royal Navy. Moreover, the Ca- class proved to be practically repetitions of the "Z" class; the heavy directors were not fitted and they had eight tubes.

When completed, these destroyers displaced about 1,700 tons but this has been increased to just over 2,000 tons after modernization. All except the Ca- boats are of all welded construction, the *Contest* being the first destroyer to be completed thus for the Royal Navy. The original armament was four 4·5-inch dual purpose guns, mounted singly, and four torpedo tubes (eight in the Ca- boats). They were the last British destroyers with their main armament in single mountings and open shields. The Ca- class had hand-worked guns but the remainder were power-worked.

Between 1954–59, all surviving boats were modified as A/S escorts; X gun was replaced by squids and the Ca- class lost their after set of tubes. The *Chaplet, Chieftain, Comet* and *Contest* are also fitted for minelaying. Y gun and all tubes have been removed from these boats. The Ca- boats have undergone extensive modernization.

Dimensions: 362·75 × 35·7 × 10 feet. 40,000 h.p. = 33 knots. Complement 186. (*Plate Nos.* 110 *and* 111)

	Builder	Launched
CAESAR (ex-*Ranger*)	Clydebank	1944
CAMBRIAN (ex-*Spitfire*)	Scott	1943
CAPRICE (ex-*Swallow*)	Yarrow	1943
CARRON (ex-*Strenuous*)	Scott	1944
CARYSFORT	White	1944
CASSANDRA (ex-*Tourmaline*)	Yarrow	1943
CAVALIER	White	1944
CAVENDISH (ex-*Sibyl*)	Clydebank	1944

	Builder	Launched	Disposal
CHAPLET	Thornycroft	1944	
CHARITY	Thornycroft	1944	Transferred to Pakistan in 1958
CHEQUERS	Scott	1944	
CHEVIOT	Stephen	1944	
CHEVRON	Stephen	1944	
CHIEFTAIN	Scott	1945	
CHILDERS	Denny	1945	
CHIVALROUS	Denny	1945	Transferred to Pakistan in 1954
COCKADE	Yarrow	1944	
COMET	Yarrow	1944	
COMUS	Thornycroft	1945	Broken up in 1958
CONCORD (ex-*Corso*)	Thornycroft	1945	
CONSORT	Stephen	1944	
CONSTANCE	Parsons/Vickers	1944	Broken up in 1956
CONTEST	White	1944	
COSSACK	Parsons/Vickers	1944	
CREOLE	White	1945	Transferred to Pakistan in 1956
CRESCENT	Clydebank	1944	Presented to Canada in 1945
CRISPIN (ex-*Craccher*)	White	1945	Transferred to Pakistan in 1956
CROMWELL (ex-*Cretan*)	Scott	1945	Sold to Norway in 1946
CROWN	Scott	1945	Sold to Norway in 1946
CROZIERS	Yarrow	1944	Sold to Norway in 1946
CRUSADER	Clydebank	1944	Presented to Canada in 1945
CRYSTAL	Yarrow	1945	Sold to Norway in 1946

THE "BATTLE" CLASSES

IN the 1942 programme it was proposed to build two flotillas of fleet destroyers and three flotillas of the intermediate type. It was originally proposed to name the new fleet destroyers with "A" and "B" names but when it was found that they were to be comparable to the "Tribals", it was felt that a more distinctive set of names would be preferable and the choice fell upon a series of naval and land engagements. All the earlier names were those of naval battles but later names also included land actions. The intermediate destroyers of the programme became the "C" classes, already listed.

In the 1942 and 1943 programmes there were to have been five flotillas of "Battles", designed for service in the Pacific, but in the end, only three flotillas were completed, two of the early type and one of an improved design. They were very strongly built and their outstanding feature was the concentration of the main armament forward, though this was much criticized as being too weak for vessels of over 2,000 tons.

A 4-inch gun (for star shell) was mounted abaft the funnel in the *Armada*, *Barfleur*, *Camperdown*, *Hogue* and *Trafalgar*, but this was removed about 1952. After the war, squids were mounted in most boats.

The later group differed from the earlier boats by having a fifth 4·7-inch gun mounted amidships, and quintuple tubes. They had heavier directors. In all classes the main armament was radar-controlled.

In 1959, the *Agincourt*, *Alamein*, *Barrosa* and *Corunna* were taken in hand for conversion into radar pickets.

Details for both classes are very much the same. The early "Battles" displace 2,315 tons; the later ones 2,460 tons. Dimensions for all: 355 × 40·5 × 12·75 feet. 50,000 h.p. = 35·75 knots. Complements vary between 230 and 300.

The early "Battles"

ARMADA   SAINTES   SOLEBAY

Built by Hawthorn Leslie. The *Armada* was launched in 1943, the others in 1944. (*Plate No.* 112)

BARFLEUR   GABBARD   ST. KITTS   TRAFALGAR

Built by Swan Hunter. The *Barfleur* was launched in 1943, the *St. Kitts* and *Trafalgar* in 1944 and the *Gabbard* in 1945. The *Gabbard* was sold to Pakistan in 1956.

CADIZ   CAMPERDOWN   FINISTERRE   ST. JAMES   VIGO

Built by Fairfield. The first three were launched in 1944, the other two in 1945. The *Cadiz* was sold to Pakistan in 1956.

GRAVELINES   HOGUE   LAGOS   SLUYS

Built by Cammell Laird. The first three were launched in 1944, the *Sluys* in 1945.

The later "Battles"

AGINCOURT   ALAMEIN

Launched by Hawthorn Leslie in 1945. (*Plate No.* 113)

AISNE

Launched by Vickers-Armstrong in 1945.

BARROSA   MATAPAN

Launched at Clydebank in 1945.

CORUNNA

Launched by Swan Hunter in 1945.

DUNKIRK   JUTLAND (ex-*Malplaquet*)

Built by Stephen. The *Dunkirk* was launched in 1945; the *Jutland* in 1946. The original *Jutland*, launched by Hawthorn Leslie in 1945, was suspended.

The following "Battle" class destroyers were launched but not completed, being scrapped or used for special trials:
Albuera, Jutland, Namur, Navarino, Oudenarde and *Talavera.*

THE "WEAPON" CLASS

THESE four monstrosities, survivors of two flotillas of which only 13 were laid down, represent the penultimate word in destroyers and were intended to be fast A/S escorts with emphasis on A/S equipment rather than surface armament. The foremost funnel is situated inside the lattice mast while the after funnel is an insignificant affair. The original design, with two funnels in the conventional positions and six guns in twin mountings, was quite handsome, but the present one, especially after conversion to radar pickets, makes them the most hideous war vessels ever built for the Royal Navy.

They are of 2,000 tons, yet mount only four 4-inch guns in two mountings. As completed, the *Broadsword* and *Battleaxe* had their guns fore and aft with the squids forward. The other two had their guns forward and the squids aft. They had ten torpedo tubes. In 1958–59, all were converted into radar pickets and they now have a large radar aerial mounted on a lattice tower amidships, guns mounted in the A and B positions and the squids aft. All torpedo tubes have been removed.

Their dimensions are 341·5 × 38 × 12·75 feet. 40,000 h.p. = 34 knots. Complement 234.

BATTLEAXE   BROADSWORD

Launched by Yarrow in 1945 and 1946 respectively.

CROSSBOW

Launched by Thornycroft in 1945. (*Plate No.* 114)

H*

SCORPION (ex-*Tomahawk*, ex-*Centaur*)

Launched by White in 1946. She was given her present name as a compliment to Lord Cunningham of Hyndhope who had commanded the *Scorpion* of 1910 for seven years. A Scorpion was an ancient weapon, a kind of scourge, armed with metal points, and also a siege engine of the ballista type.

THE *DARING* CLASS

UNDER the 1944 programme, two flotillas of a modified "Battle" class were to be built; a flotilla of a modified "Weapon" class was also provided for.

The modified "Battles" were given "D" names and the "Weapons" were to be the "G" class. In 1945, however, it was decided to proceed with one flotilla only of the "D's" and none at all of the "G" class. The Ships' Names Committee then selected the eight best names and the *Daring* class came into existence.

Though built as destroyers, these vessels were later officially described as the "*Daring* class ships" thus becoming neither fish, nor fowl, nor good red herring! They have now become destroyers again.

They displace 2,610 tons, with dimensions 390 × 43 × 12·75 feet. 54,000 h.p. = 34·75 knots. Their complements vary, but average about 300. They have six 4·5-inch guns and ten torpedo tubes.

The "Weapon" appearance has been repeated, though for a few years the *Daring* and *Diana* had a larger, and raking, casing fitted to the second funnel which did something to improve their appearance. This was removed in 1957.

These ships are extremely handy and have a very small turning circle. They are capable of performing a variety of functions equally well, including reconnaissance, A/A and A/S duties.

The after set of torpedo tubes has been removed and a deck-house built instead.

DAINTY

Launched by White in 1950.

129. *CAMPBELL*, 1932

130. *CODRINGTON*, 1939

131. *KEMPENFELT, 1932*

132. *GRENVILLE, 1937*

DARING

Launched by Swan Hunter in 1949.

DECOY   DIANA

Launched by Yarrow in 1949 and 1952 respectively.

DEFENDER

Launched by Stephen in 1950.

DELIGHT

Launched by Fairfield in 1950. (*Plate No.* 115)

DIAMOND

Launched at Clydebank in 1950.

DUCHESS

Launched by Thornycroft in 1951.

THE "HUNT" CLASS

THOUGH these boats were later known as Frigates, they were built as destroyers and therefore should come within the scope of this book. Eighty-six were built, the first being laid down in 1939 and the last in 1941.

Their function was escorting, not fleet work, but they were tough little ships and very good indeed for their size. They were employed as convoy escorts on the East Coast, in the Channel, in the Arctic and in the Mediterranean, but it was only the chronic shortage of larger escorts that caused them to be used on long trips such as the Russian Convoys, for their endurance was limited and they had to refuel at sea too often, especially if they used high speeds which were often necessary on escort duty.

They were not really up to fleet screening on account of their relatively low speed and small size which cut them down in a seaway so that it was hard to keep up without damage. But they were magnificent A/S ships; manœuvrable, fast and with quick acceleration. The A/A armament of the Type II and onward was very good and they gave as good as they got.

Four distinct types were built, the first being 1,000 tons, but they carried four 4-inch guns only, instead of the designed six. This was due to the fact that they were found to be unstable and had to surrender a good deal of top weight, including one twin mounting; their funnels were cut down also.

Type II, of which there were 33 originally, had six 4-inch guns and were of 1,050 tons. The errors made in the Type I design were corrected. It is probable that these were the most successful of all the "Hunts". While still on the stocks, the Type II "Hunts" had an extra plate added on each side of the keel which increased their beam by about two feet. It produced a stiff, sturdy seaboat but as the propellers were each one foot farther away from the rudder, some handling problems were presented.

Type III, 28 in number, were of 1,050 tons. These boats had only four 4-inch guns but mounted two torpedo tubes for offensive operations against enemy convoys.

Type IV, of which there were only two, were of Thornycroft design and quite different from the others. They mounted six 4-inch guns and three torpedo tubes. As the builders were not permitted to construct special machinery, these larger boats were two knots slower than the other types.

The first three types were all much the same in dimensions. 280 × 29 × 7·75 feet. 19,000 h.p. = 27 knots.

It is a point of interest that the "Hunts" were fitted with stabilizers. These were not popular with the commanding officers for several reasons:

(a) They filled a valuable space which might have been used as a fuel tank.

(b) This space had to be kept open when the stabilizers were working thereby prejudicing the watertight integrity of the ship.

(c) They required a great deal of electric power to operate them and this affected the radar most adversely.

(d) They did not do much to stabilize the ship except in a beam sea or with the sea on the bow. If the ship was steaming into a head sea, the fins broke surface and strained the ship as a result. With a sea on the quarter there was an alarming tendency to broach to.

It is believed that in later boats the stabilizers were taken out and the space used as a fuel tank.

I am indebted to certain officers, who commanded "Hunts" during the war, for much of the above information.

(Plate No. 116)

TYPE I

	Builder	*Launched*	*Disposal*
ATHERSTONE	Cammell Laird	1939	Broken up in 1958
BERKELEY	Cammell Laird	1940	Disabled by air attack and sunk by our own forces in 1942 during the Dieppe Raid
CATTISTOCK	Yarrow	1940	Broken up in 1958
CLEVELAND	Yarrow	1940	
COTSWOLD	Yarrow	1940	Became a breakwater at Harwich *c.* 1956
COTTESMORE	Yarrow	1940	Sold to Egypt in 1950
EGLINTON	Vickers-Armstrong	1939	
EXMOOR	Vickers-Armstrong	1940	Sunk by an E-boat in 1941
FERNIE	Clydebank	1940	Broken up in 1957
GARTH	Clydebank	1940	Broken up in 1958
HAMBLEDON	Swan Hunter	1939	Is now part of an artificial harbour
HOLDERNESS	Swan Hunter	1940	Broken up in 1956
MENDIP	Swan Hunter	1940	Lent to China in 1948–49. Sold to Egypt in 1949
MEYNELL	Swan Hunter	1940	Sold to Ecuador in 1955
PYTCHLEY	Scott	1940	Broken up in 1957
QUANTOCK	Scott	1940	Sold to Ecuador in 1955
QUORN	White	1940	Sunk by a mine or human torpedo in 1944, off Normandy
SOUTHDOWN	White	1940	Broken up in 1957
TYNEDALE	Stephen	1940	Sunk by a U-boat in 1943
WHADDON	Stephen	1940	Broken up in 1958

Details of Type I

1,000 tons. 280 × 29 × 7·75 feet. 19,000 h.p. = 27·5 knots. Four 4-inch. No torpedo tubes. Complement 146.

(Plate No. 117*)*

TYPE II

	Builder	Launched	Disposal
AVON VALE	Clydebank	1940	Broken up in 1958
BADSWORTH	Cammell Laird	1941	Sold to Norway in 1944
BEAUFORT	Cammell Laird	1941	Transferred to Norway in 1952
BEDALE	Hawthorn Leslie	1941	Lent to India in 1953
BICESTER	Hawthorn Leslie	1941	Broken up in 1959
BLACKMORE	Stephen	1941	Lent to Denmark in 1952
BLANKNEY	Clydebank	1941	Sank four U-boats 1941–44
BRAMHAM	Stephen	1941	Transferred to Greece in 1946
CALPE	Swan Hunter	1941	Lent to Denmark in 1952
CHIDDINGFOLD	Scott	1941	Transferred to India in 1953
COWDRAY	Scott	1941	
CROOME	Stephen	1941	Broken up in 1957
DULVERTON	Stephen	1941	Sunk by a glider bomb off Kos in 1943
ERIDGE	Swan Hunter	1940	Sold in 1947
EXMOOR (ex-*Burton*)	Swan Hunter	1941	Lent to Denmark in 1953
FARNDALE	Swan Hunter	1940	
GROVE	Swan Hunter	1941	Sunk by a U-boat in 1942
HEYTHROP	Swan Hunter	1940	Sunk by a U-boat in 1942
HURSLEY	Swan Hunter	1941	Transferred to Greece in 1943
HURWORTH	Vickers-Armstrong	1941	Sunk by mine in 1943
LAMERTON	Swan Hunter	1940	Transferred to India in 1953
LAUDERDALE	Thornycroft	1941	Transferred to Greece in 1946
LEDBURY	Thornycroft	1941	Broken up in 1958
MIDDLETON	Vickers-Armstrong	1941	Became a pontoon at Harwich in 1956

OAKLEY	Vickers-Armstrong	1940	Lent to Poland in 1941 and sunk by a mine in 1942
OAKLEY (ex-*Tickham*)	Yarrow	1942	Sold to Federal Germany in 1958
PUCKERIDGE	White	1941	Sunk by a U-boat in 1943
SILVERTON	White	1940	Broken up in 1958
SOUTHWOLD	White	1941	Sunk by a mine in 1942
TETCOTT	White	1941	Broken up in 1956
WHEATLAND	Yarrow	1941	Became a pontoon at Harwich in 1956
WILTON	Yarrow	1941	
ZETLAND	Yarrow	1942	Transferred to Norway in 1952

Details of Type II

1,050 tons. 280 × 31·5 × 7·8 feet. 19,000 h.p. = 27 knots. Six 4-inch. No torpedo tubes. Complement 146.

(*Plate No.* 118)

TYPE III

	Builder	*Launched*	*Disposal*
AIREDALE	Clydebank	1941	Sunk by aircraft in the Eastern Mediterranean in 1942
ALBRIGHTON	Clydebank	1941	Sold to Federal Germany in 1958
ALDENHAM	Cammell Laird	1941	Sunk by a mine in 1944
BELVOIR	Cammell Laird	1941	Broken up in 1957
BLEAN	Hawthorn Leslie	1942	Torpedoed by a U-boat in 1942
BLEASDALE	Vickers-Armstrong	1941	Broken up in 1956
BOLEBROKE	Swan Hunter	1941	Transferred to Greece in 1946
BORDER	Swan Hunter	1942	Lent to Greece and broken up on return in 1945
CATTERICK	Vickers-Armstrong	1941	Transferred to Greece in 1946

	Builder	Launched	Disposal
DERWENT	Vickers-Armstrong	1941	Broken up in 1946
EASTON	White	1942	
EGGESFORD	White	1942	Sold to Federal Germany in 1958
GLAISDALE	Cammell Laird	1942	Transferred to Norway in 1944
GOATHLAND	Fairfield	1942	Broken up in 1946
HALDON	Fairfield	1942	Lent to Free French and sunk by a mine in 1944
HATHERLEIGH	Vickers-Armstrong	1941	Transferred to Greece on completion
HAYDON	Vickers-Armstrong	1942	Broken up in 1958
HOLCOMB	Stephen	1942	Sunk by a U-boat in 1943
LIMBOURNE	Stephen	1942	Torpedoed by an E-boat in 1943 and sunk by our own forces
MELBREAK	Swan Hunter	1942	Broken up in 1956
MODBURY	Swan Hunter	1942	Broken up in 1956
PENYLAN	Vickers-Armstrong	1942	Sunk by an E-boat in 1942
ROCKWOOD	Vickers-Armstrong	1942	Broken up in 1946
STEVENSTONE	White	1942	
TALYBONT	White	1943	
TANATSIDE	Yarrow	1942	Transferred to Greece in 1946
WENSLEYDALE	Yarrow	1942	Broken up in 1946

Details of Type III

1,050 tons. 280 × 31·5 × 7·8 feet. 19,000 h.p. = 27 knots. Four 4-inch. Two torpedo tubes. Complement 168.

TYPE IV

BRECON   BRISSENDEN

Both launched by Thornycroft in 1942. 1,175 tons. 283 × 34 × 9 feet. 19,000 h.p. = 25 knots. Six 4-inch. Three torpedo tubes. Complement 170. These two boats were described as "The shape of things to come". The abandoning of the structurally unsound forecastle break amidships, in favour of the shelter deck, was a departure from the conventional which seemed to the builders long overdue. It transformed inherent weakness into a tower of strength.

The shelter deck was introduced at the time with two main points in view, viz. getting rid of a weak spot and gaining internal access to any part of the ship. These two points were fully achieved; not only was the weak spot eliminated but the longitudinal stresses—tensile and compressive—were so reduced as to render the use of H.T. steel unnecessary and mild steel was used instead.

It is of interest to see that modern frigate design follows the above ideas.

The funnels of these two boats, in plan view as seen from above, were pear-shaped in appearance and were thus shaped to facilitate the formation of a satisfactory smoke plume and to minimize downward flow of smoke on to the decks under all conditions of speed and wind.

A central division plate, twisted in the form of a spiral, was fitted in these funnels. The purpose of this was to prevent aircraft flying overhead from picking up the glow from the boiler furnaces at night.

The above information about these two interesting destroyers was most kindly supplied by the builders, John I. Thornycroft & Co. Ltd. (*Plate No.* 119)

THE AMERICAN DESTROYERS

IN 1940, the United States gave us fifty old destroyers, built between 1917 and 1920, in exchange for certain bases in British colonial territory on a 99 years lease.

These boats, while making a valuable addition to our escort forces, were not all in the best condition and gave a good deal of trouble. The American Sonar sets were not as efficient as our Asdics but they were quite useful and certainly helped to bridge the gap until the new construction came along.

They were renamed after towns and villages common to the United Kingdom (or Commonwealth) and the United States. Some were traditional.

On transfer, these "four-stackers" had their three aftermost funnels cut down a little in most cases, but the foremost one remained at its original height. The *Lincoln, Ludlow* and *Leeds* always had three funnels and the *Bradford*, on transfer, only two. Certain others had two funnels removed during the war.

They were of several different classes, but in general the displacement was something over 1,000 tons and they were about 300 × 30 × 7 feet. When they were transferred they mounted four 4-inch guns and twelve torpedo tubes in triple mounts. This armament was considerably altered after transfer to the Royal Navy; at first they had three 4-inch and one 12-pounder H.A. but after 1943 two of the 4-inch were taken out. Two to four Oerlikons were fitted about 1942. The *Lewes, Leeds* and *Ludlow,* after 1943, mounted two 3-inch guns. They had no forward 4-inch.

In the list which follows, the original U.S. names are given and the boats which served in the R.C.N. are also mentioned. Notes about funnels and clinker screens on the foremost funnel are given for the sake of completeness. (*Plate Nos.* 120, 121, 122 *and* 123)

ANNAPOLIS (ex-*Mackenzie*)	R.C.N. Sold in 1945
BATH (ex-*Hopewell*)	Manned by the Norwegians in 1941 and sunk in the same year
BELMONT (ex-*Satterlee*)	Torpedoed in 1942
BEVERLEY (ex-*Branch*)	Sunk by a U-boat in 1943
BRADFORD (ex-*McLanahan*)	Converted into a long-range escort, with two funnels, in 1941. Broken up in 1946
BRIGHTON (ex-*Cowell*)	Transferred to Russia in 1944. Returned and broken up in 1949
BROADWATER (ex-*Mason*)	Sunk by a U-boat in 1941
BROADWAY (ex-*Hunt*)	Had a clinker screen on foremost funnel. Sold in 1947
BURNHAM (ex-*Aulick*)	Broken up in 1938
BURWELL (ex-*Laub*)	Broken up in 1947
BUXTON (ex-*Edwards*)	Sold in Canada in 1946
CALDWELL (ex-*Hale*)	Broken up in 1945
CAMERON (ex-*Welles*)	Bombed in dock at Portsmouth in 1940. Not given as an official war loss but used for shock trials. Broken up in 1944
CAMPBELTOWN (ex-*Buchanan*)	At first manned by Polish Navy but returned. Expended as an assault ship at St. Nazaire in 1942
CASTLETON (ex-*Aaron Ward*)	Broken up in 1947

CHARLESTOWN (ex-*Abbot*)	Broken up in 1947
CHELSEA (ex-*Crowninshield*)	Lent to Russia in 1944. Returned and broken up in 1949
CHESTERFIELD (ex-*Wood*)	Broken up in 1948
CHURCHILL (ex-*Herndon*)	Had a clinker screen on foremost funnel. Lent to Russia in 1944 and torpedoed in 1945 while in Russian service
CLARE (ex-*Upsher*)	Had two funnels only. Sold in 1945
COLUMBIA (ex-*Haraden*)	R.C.N. Sold in 1945
GEORGETOWN (ex-*Maddox*)	Lent to Russia in 1944. Returned and broken up in 1952
HAMILTON (ex-*Kalk*)	R.C.N. Sold in 1945
LANCASTER (ex-*Philip*)	Broken up in 1947
LEAMINGTON (ex-*Twiggs*)	Lent to Russia in 1944. Returned in 1950 and broken up in 1951
LEEDS (ex-*Conner*)	Three funnels. Sold in 1947
LEWES (ex-*Conway*)	Sold in Australia in 1946
LINCOLN (ex-*Yarnall*)	Three funnels. Given to Russia as a gift for cannibalization to provide spares for the rest of the flotilla in 1944. Returned in 1952 and broken up
LUDLOW (ex-*Stockton*)	Three funnels. Sold in 1945
MANSFIELD (ex-*Evans*)	Manned by Norwegians in 1941–42. Loaned to R.C.N. in 1942 and broken up in Canada in 1944
MONTGOMERY (ex-*Wickes*)	Broken up in 1945
NEWARK (ex-*Ringgold*)	Broken up in 1947
NEWMARKET (ex-*Robinson*)	Broken up in 1946
NEWPORT (ex-*Sigourney*)	Manned by Norwegians in 1941–42. Broken up in 1947
NIAGARA (ex-*Thatcher*)	R.C.N. Disposed of in 1946
RAMSEY (ex-*Meade*)	Broken up in 1947
READING (ex-*Bailey*)	Broken up in 1945
RICHMOND (ex-*Fairfax*)	Lent to Russia in 1944. Returned in 1949 and broken up
RIPLEY (ex-*Shubrick*)	Had a clinker screen on foremost funnel. Broken up in 1945
ROCKINGHAM (ex-*Swasey*)	Sunk by mine in 1944

ROXBOROUGH (ex-*Foote*)	Lent to Russia in 1944. Returned in 1949 and broken up
ST. ALBANS (ex-*Thomas*)	Lent to Russia in 1944. Returned in 1949 and broken up
ST. CLAIR (ex-*William*)	R.C.N. Sold in Canada in 1946
ST. CROIX (ex-*McCook*)	R.C.N. Torpedoed in 1945
ST. FRANCIS (ex-*Bancroft*)	R.C.N. Sold in Canada in 1945
ST. MARYS (ex-*Doran*)	Broken up in 1945
SALISBURY (ex-*Claxton*)	Lent to R.C.N. in 1942. Sold in Canada in 1944
SHERWOOD (ex-*Rodgers*)	Pronounced worn out in 1943 and gutted. Beached as a rocket target
STANLEY (ex-*McAlla*)	Two funnels. Sunk by a U-boat in 1941
WELLS (ex-*Tillman*)	Broken up in 1946

FLOTILLA LEADERS

THE life of the flotilla leader as a separate type was a short one, only about twenty years in fact. While fleet flotillas had a speed of about 27 knots, the Captain (D) and his staff were accommodated in a light cruiser. The "Gem" class cruisers with a speed of about 22 knots were later replaced by the "Scouts" of 25 knots. Later, the light cruisers of the *Boadicea* class were employed and their speed was slightly more. At Heligoland, in 1914, Commodore Tyrrwhit led the "L" destroyers of the Harwich Force in the 28-knot *Arethusa*.

With the coming of the "M" class destroyers with their higher speeds, it was decided to build a new type known as the flotilla leader, the first of which were the *Marksman* class. Their speed was 34 knots and they were merely large destroyers with more accommodation for the Captain (D) and his staff.

The first leader ever built was not designed as such, indeed, it is hard to know exactly why she was built. This was the *Swift*, launched by Cammell Laird in 1907. She acted in various capacities, including that of leader. She was a remarkable boat, designed for 35 knots and credited with 38 knots on trials.

Then, in 1914, four large destroyers building for the Chilean Navy were taken over, renamed and used as leaders. These were the four *Broke* class.

Under the 1913–14 estimates, two destroyers were lengthened and re-designed as leaders. These were the *Marksman* and the *Nimrod*. Two more, the *Lightfoot* and *Kempenfelt*, were built under the 1914–15 estimates and three more under the emergency war programme.

Then followed the six leaders of the *Grenville* class, the eight *Bruce* class and five *Broke* class. After the war there was a lull and it was 1929 before the next leader was launched. This was the *Codrington*, a magnificent boat of 2,000 tons which was the leader of the "A" class destroyers.

After this, each flotilla of eight had its leader, a slightly enlarged edition of the class and not as big as the *Codrington*. With the coming of the "J" class, the leaders were included in the flotillas and were merely destroyers fitted for the accommodation of the Captain (D). No more leaders, as a separate type, were built. Their names, however, signified their status and the additional accommodation increased their displacement by a small amount.

The "between wars" leaders were not large enough to hold the whole of the Captain (D)'s staff so that various members were accommodated in the boats of the flotilla. During the Second World War the flotilla leaders served mostly as private ships except in the fleet flotillas.

SWIFT

Launched by Cammell Laird in 1907. 2,207 tons. 345 × 34·3 × 12·5 feet. Complement 130. 30,000 h.p. = 35 knots. Four 4-inch. Two torpedo tubes. Yarrow boilers.

For several years her mainmast was considerably higher than the foremast but during the war a fore-topmast was fitted, raking slightly forward which detracted greatly from her appearance. Later in the war, the two foremost 4-inch guns were replaced by a 6-inch. This was subsequently removed.

She served with the 1st Flotilla until 1912 and then was attached to a battle squadron and the fleet flagship for eighteen months. She became leader of the 4th Flotilla in 1913 and spent most of the war in the Dover Patrol. She was sold in 1921. (*Plate No.* 124)

BOTHA (ex-*Almirante Robelledo*)   BROKE (ex-*Almirante Goni*)
FAULKNOR (ex-*Almirante Simpson*)   TIPPERARY (ex-*Almirante Riveros*)

All built by White, the first three being launched in 1913 and the *Tipperary* in 1915. Just over 1,700 tons. 320 × 32·5 × 11·6 feet. 30,000 h.p. = 31–32 knots. White-Forster boilers. Six 4-inch. Three torpedo tubes. In 1918 the surviving boats were rearmed with two 4·7-inch and two 4-inch guns and four torpedo tubes. Complement 205. The *Tipperary* was sunk at Jutland and the others were sold to Chile in 1920. They had good officer accommodation but indifferent crew space. (*Plate No.* 125)

	Builder	Launched	Disposal
ABDIEL	Cammell Laird	1915	Sold in 1927
GABRIEL	Cammell Laird	1915	Sold in 1921
ITHURIEL	Cammell Laird	1915	Sold in 1921
KEMPENFELT	Cammell Laird	1915	Sold in 1921
LIGHTFOOT	White	1915	Sold in 1921
MARKSMAN	Hawthorn Leslie	1915	Sold in 1921
NIMROD	Denny	1915	Sold in 1925

They were all between 1,600 and 1,700 tons. 315 × 31·75 × 12·3 feet. Complement 105. 36,000 h.p. = 34 knots. Four 4-inch. Four torpedo tubes. All had Yarrow boilers except the *Lightfoot* which had White-Forster.

The *Abdiel* was a minelayer and carried 80 mines. She had no torpedo tubes and only one 4-inch gun, though a second was mounted after the war. She was the only one in which the foremost funnel was not heightened. The *Gabriel* became a minelayer in 1918. (*Plate No.* 126)

In 1917, the *Lightfoot* and *Nimrod*, serving with the Harwich Force, were fitted with two 14-inch torpedo tubes, one on either beam, under the midship gun platform. They were intended for use at night and had only a short range. They were taken out after the war.

	Builder	Launched	Disposal
ANZAC	Denny	1917	Transferred to the R.A.N. in 1919 and sold in 1935
GRENVILLE	Cammell Laird	1916	Sold in 1931
HOSTE	Cammell Laird	1916	Sunk in collision with H.M.S. *Negro* in 1916
PARKER (ex-*Frobisher*)	Cammell Laird	1916	Sold in 1921
SAUMAREZ	Cammell Laird	1916	Sold in 1930
SEYMOUR	Cammell Laird	1916	Sold in 1929

In this class the bridge was moved aft and the uptakes from the two foremost boilers were brought up into one large casing which detracted very much from their appearance. Superfiring guns were mounted forward, a system later installed in the "V" and "W" destroyers. The *Anzac* had the forecastle raised by one foot.

They were of about 1,670 tons. 325 × 31·75 × 11 feet. 36,500 h.p. = 34 knots. Four 4-inch. Four torpedo tubes. Yarrow boilers. Complement 126. (*Plate No.* 127)

Thornycroft leaders

In 1916, the Commander-in-Chief Grand Fleet having asked for larger leaders, two new types were laid down, one to Thornycroft design and the other to Admiralty specifications. These were intended as leaders for the "V" and "W" destroyers. Two of the Thornycroft boats were laid down in 1916, one in 1917 and two more in 1918. The last two, *Keppel* and *Rooke* (renamed *Broke* in 1921) lay in Royal Dockyards for several years before they were finally completed in 1925 and 1924 respectively. Contracts for two more (*Saunders* and *Spragge*) were cancelled.

These boats appeared very large on account of their high freeboard and their big, flat-sided funnels.

1,740 tons. 329 × 31·8 × 13 feet. 40,000 h.p. = 36 knots. (37–38 knots on trials). Yarrow boilers. Five 4·7-inch. One 3-inch. Six torpedo tubes. Complement 183.

During the Second World War, most of these boats had their after funnels cut down and their armament reduced.

(*Plate No.* 128)

	Launched	Disposal
BROKE (ex-*Rooke*)	1920	Sunk by gunfire of shore batteries at Algiers in 1942
KEPPEL	1920	At the sinking of five U-boats, 1943–44. Broken up in 1946
SHAKESPEARE	1917	Sold in 1936
SPENSER (ex-*Spencer*)	1917	Sold in 1936
WALLACE	1918	Converted into a "Wair" in 1939. Broken up in 1946

Admiralty design

	Builder	Launched	Disposal
BRUCE	Cammell Laird	1918	Sunk as a target in 1939
CAMPBELL	Cammell Laird	1918	Broken up in 1948
DOUGLAS	Cammell Laird	1918	Broken up in 1946
MACKAY	Cammell Laird	1918	Broken up in 1946
MALCOLM	Cammell Laird	1918	Broken up in 1946
MONTROSE	Hawthorn Leslie	1918	Broken up in 1945
SCOTT	Cammell Laird	1917	Sunk by a U-boat in 1918
STUART	Hawthorn Leslie	1918	Transferred to the R.A.N. in 1933

1,800 tons. 332·5 × 31·8 × 13 feet. 40,000 h.p. = 36·5 knots. Yarrow boilers. Complement 183. Five 4·7-inch. One 3-inch. Six torpedo tubes.

These, together with the Thornycroft boats, were the leaders of our running flotillas for a number of years after the First World War. (*Plate No.* 129)

CODRINGTON

Launched by Swan Hunter in 1929. 1,540 tons. 332 × 33·75 × 12.25 feet. 39,000 h.p. = 35 knots. Admiralty boilers. Five 4·7-inch. Eight torpedo tubes. Complement 185. Sunk by bombing in Dover Harbour in 1940.

The remaining leaders were all merely enlarged editions, with additional accommodation, of the destroyers of the "B" to "I" classes. The *Keith* and *Kempenfelt* were leaders of the "B" and "C" flotillas; the others had names beginning with their class letter. (*Plate No.* 130)

	Builder	Launched	Disposal
KEITH	Vickers-Armstrong	1930	Sunk by bombing at Dunkirk in 1940
KEMPENFELT	White	1931	Transferred to the R.C.N. in 1939
DUNCAN	Portsmouth Dockyard	1932	Sank three U-boats in 1943 Broken up in 1946
EXMOUTH	Portsmouth Dockyard	1934	Torpedoed in 1940

	Builder	Launched	Disposal
FAULKNOR	Yarrow	1934	Sank three U-boats 1939–42. Broken up in 1946
GRENVILLE	Yarrow	1935	Sunk by a mine in 1940
HARDY	Cammell Laird	1936	Driven ashore and abandoned at Narvik in 1940
INGLEFIELD	Cammell Laird	1936	Sunk by a glider bomb off Anzio in 1944

These leaders varied in displacement from 1,400 to 1,530 tons, each one being slightly larger than her predecessor. The first three had four 4·7-inch guns; the others had five. All except the *Inglefield*, which had ten, mounted eight torpedo tubes. The complement in all was 175. Their average dimensions were 326 × 33 × 8·7 feet. Their horse power ranged from 36,000 to 38,000 giving about 36 knots. (*Plate Nos.* 131 *and* 132)

INDEX

Italic figures indicate illustration numbers